A Guide to Psychologists and Their Concepts

A Series of Books in Psychology

Editors:

Richard C. Atkinson
Jonathan Freedman
Gardner Lindzey
Richard F. Thompson

A Guide to Psychologists and Their Concepts

Vernon J. Nordby and Calvin S. Hall

W. H. Freeman and Company
San Francisco

Our grateful acknowledgments go to Richard Coan and John Flavell. We especially thank Henry Benson for the portraits that adorn this book.

Library of Congress Cataloging in Publication Data

Nordby, Vernon J.
A guide to psychologists and their concepts.

1. Psychologists—Biography. 2. Psychology.
I. Hall, Calvin Springer, 1909- II. Title.
[DNLM: 1. Psychology—Biography. 2. Psychology—History. BF109.A1 N828g]
BF109.A1N67 150'.92'2 [B] 74-11165
ISBN 0-7167-0760-8
ISBN 0-7167-0759-4 (pbk.)

Printed in the United States of America

9 8 7 6 5 4 3 2

To Carl and Betty

Contents

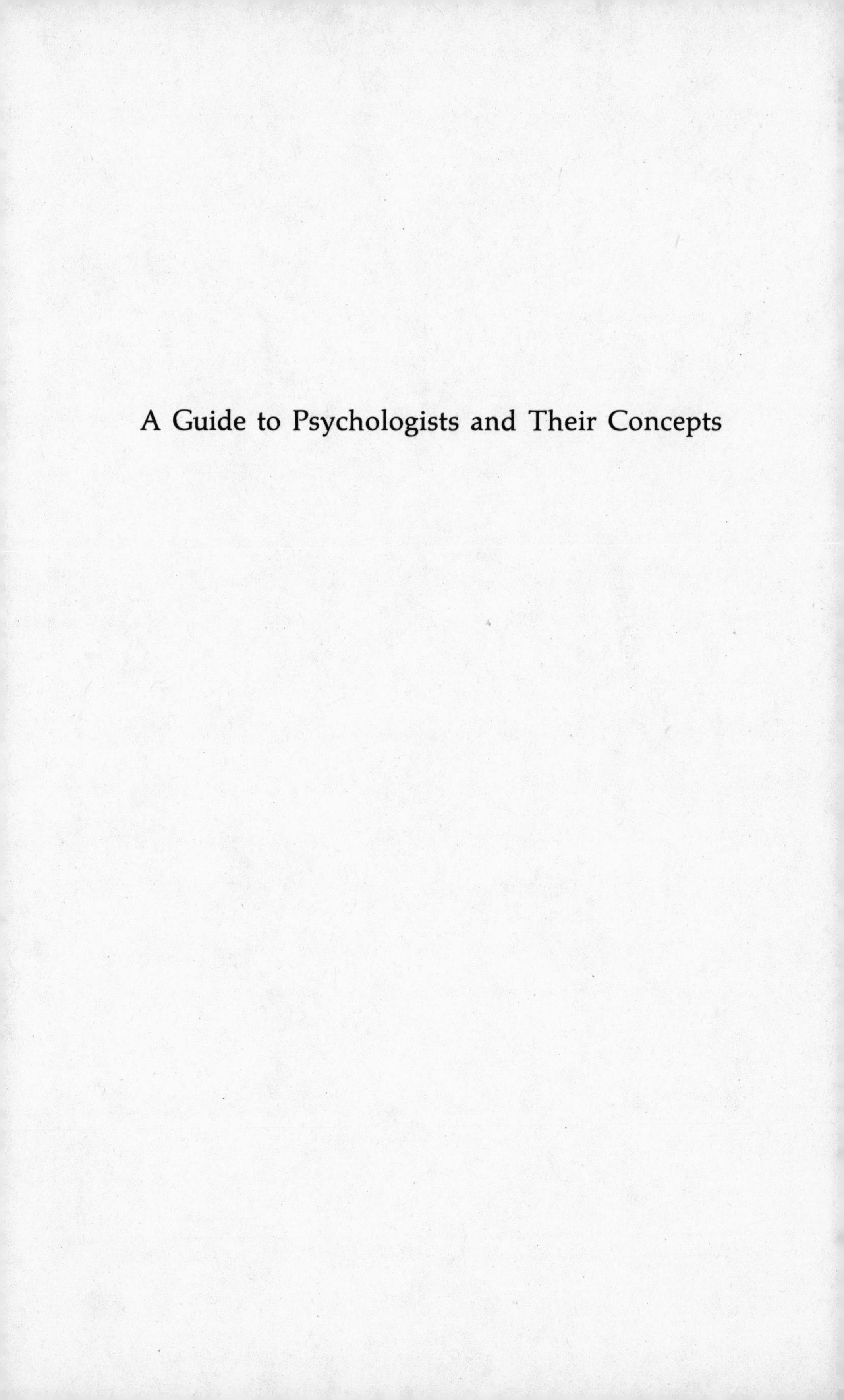

A Guide to Psychologists and Their Concepts

Introduction

The aims of this book are twofold: first, to present brief biographies of persons whose thinking has been influential and sometimes decisive in establishing the conceptual horizons of contemporary psychology; second, to set forth as clearly and as succinctly as we can their principal concepts. This guide is written for the general reader and for the student with a minimal background in psychology. It may also serve as a handy reference for the more advanced student and for the instructor.

Two critical decisions had to be made in planning the guide. What psychologists should be included, and which of their concepts should be described?

The main criterion we followed in choosing the psychologists is that their ideas should be viable and influential in the contemporary psychological scene. By this criterion some important historical figures were eliminated. We have also omitted psychologists whose concepts are clearly borrowed or derived from theories developed by others, even though many of these are experimental and applied psychologists who have made substantial and valuable contributions to experimental design and methodology, to the practical applications of psychological principles in psychotherapy, education, industry, community health, and many other areas, to the testing of hypotheses derived from various theories, and to the accumulation of dependable knowledge, which, after all, is the ultimate goal of a scientific psychology. Their omission from this guide is not to be construed as a reflection upon the impact their work has had upon present-day psychology. Good theory is solidly founded on observation and experiment, but also good research is the response to good theory.

Surely there will be objections to the list of psychologists we finally selected. It will be objected that some psychologists who have been included should have been omitted, and vice versa. Such criticisms are inevitable, and will undoubtedly be based on valid reasons. We will be glad to take these criticisms into consideration in planning a second edition of this guide. Nevertheless, we feel that any cross section of psychologists would have made a selection very similar to the one we have made. Moreover, we have been guided by the findings of Richard Coan, who has been conducting surveys of the influence of psychologists, and who very generously made available to us unpublished data he has collected.

Although the list of psychologists may appear to be overweighted with American psychologists, actually 19 of the 42 psychologists are European, some of them having migrated to the United States after establishing their reputations in Europe. It is also of interest that 13 of the 42 are medical doctors, many of whom specialized in psychiatry, and that 26 were born in the nineteenth century, 16 in this one. Virtually every field of psychology is represented: sensation and perception, learning, motivation and emotion, physiological, social, personality, tests and measurements, educational, and clinical. Purely statistical concepts are not included, however. And of the 42, 25 are experimental psychologists who worked in the laboratory, often using lower animals as subjects. The 42 psychologists represented in this book have generated over 400 concepts.

What is a concept? The dictionary says a concept is a general idea that has been arrived at by generalizing from particulars; the particulars, we might add, being immediate sense impressions (observations), memories, and associations. A concept is not itself an observable object; it is not a thing, but a generalization about things. It is an abstraction. One arrives at a concept of house, tree, or triangle by abstracting common features of particular houses, trees, and triangles. One difficulty with this definition of a concept is that for a man-made object, such as a house, someone must have had a concept of a house before there could be houses. Psychological concepts are clearly created by man. This suggests that concepts may be formed by insight, intuition, or imagination alone, or by the operation of inherited modes of thought without any prior observation, or by analogy with something that already exists.

Psychological concepts are generalizations about mental or behavioral phenomena. Tolman's *purpose*, Jung's *archetype*, Skinner's *positive reinforcement*, Freud's *id*, Murray's *need*, McDougall's *instinct*, Hull's *drive*, Gestalt psychology's *figure and ground*, Piaget's *assimilation*, Lewin's *vectors and valences*, Rogers' *self*, Angyal's *biosphere*, Kelly's *personal construct*, Festinger's *cognitive dissonance*, Hebb's *cell assembly*, and Erikson's *ego identity* are all generalizations about mind or behavior. Like all concepts, they are outgrowths of observation, experimental findings, inference, insight, and imagination.

Psychological concepts vary along several dimensions. Some concepts are very broad; that is, they purport to account for many kinds of behavior. Skinner's *positive reinforcement* is an example of a very broad concept. Others are more narrow, in that they deal with fewer kinds of behavior. Osgood's *semantic space* is an example of a fairly limited concept. Concepts also vary in their closeness to observational data. Freud's *id* is a fairly abstract concept, whereas Pavlov's *conditioned reflex* is closely tied to precise experimental operations. Somewhat the converse of this dimension is the ability of the concept to generate research. Some concepts, like Festinger's *cognitive dissonance*, have stimulated a lot of research; other concepts, like Jung's *archetype*, have not been as successful yet in stimulating research. Some concepts are embedded in a large, panoramic theory; other concepts stand pretty much alone. This accounts, to some degree, for the differences in the number of concepts proposed by the different psychologists represented in this guide. Panoramic theories, which attempt to encompass the whole range of psychological phenomena, are typified by those of Freud, Lewin, and Tolman.

The reader will notice that there are some similarities between concepts proposed by different psychologists, and that similar ideas are sometimes called by different names, different ideas sometimes called by the same name. This situation is unfortunate, but there is no practical remedy for it. The reader may find it interesting to look for resemblances among concepts.

There are certain concepts that all psychologists take for granted. We will not be concerned with these shared concepts. Our concern in this book is to present the distinctive and distinguishing concepts of each of the psychologists discussed.

A word about the format of this guide. The psychologists are listed alphabetically. The pages on which each of the psychologists appears are given in the table of contents. In one case, we had to combine the concepts of three men, Koffka, Köhler, and Wertheimer, under a single heading, that of Gestalt psychology, because Gestalt psychology was the joint product of their works.

The list of concepts formulated by each psychologist follows what we intend to be a logical order. In some theories, there are first-order concepts, second-order concepts, and third-order concepts. Second-order concepts are derived from first-order ones, third-order concepts from second-order ones. Headings for the first-order concepts are displayed—that is, each is printed on a line by itself. Those for the second-order concepts are flush left and run into the text under the appropriate first-order concept, and those for third-order concepts are indented under the appropriate second-order concept. The more than 400 concepts discussed in this guide are listed alphabetically in the subject index.

References are cited for each psychologist. Usually the references are selected from the psychologist's own writings, although occasionally we have put in a reference to a secondary source of information about the theory. The reader's attention is called to the following sources, which present fuller accounts of the various concepts and theories described in this guide. They are: C. S. Hall and G. Lindzey, *Theories of Personality;* E. R. Hilgard and G. Bower, *Theories of Learning;* S. Koch, ed., *Psychology: A Study of a Science;* and R. S. Woodworth and M. R. Sheehan, *Contemporary Schools of Psychology.*

Before bringing this brief introduction to a close, we would like to point out to the reader that the development of a concept is an immensely exciting and esthetically pleasing mental activity—for to form a concept is to attempt to impose order, coherence, and meaning on the myriad and often chaotic sense impressions, memories, and random thoughts that pass relentlessly through our minds. A concept is the product of contemplation, and concept invites contemplation. Science, philosophy, art, and religion represent the highest manifestations of man's need and aspiration to discover harmonious order in the universe. To find unity in diversity is a very human enterprise, to which each of the individuals represented in this guide has made a contribution. Out of their thinking and imagination have emerged the basic ideas upon which contemporary psychology is grounded.

Alfred Adler
1870–1937

Adler was an early follower of Freud's (see p. 42), but broke with him, as did Jung (see p. 95), over the issue of the importance of sexuality in human affairs. Adler held that man was primarily a social being rather than a sexual one.

Alfred Adler was born in Vienna in 1870 of a prosperous middle-class family, and died in Aberdeen, Scotland, in 1937 while on a lecture tour. Although his family was Jewish, Adler became a Protestant when he was a young man. He received a medical degree in 1895 from the University of Vienna. At first he specialized in ophthalmology, and then, after a period of practice in general medicine, he became a psychiatrist. He was one of the charter members of the Vienna Psychoanalytic Society and later its president. However, Adler soon began to develop ideas which differed from those of Freud and others in the Vienna Society, and when these differences became acute, he was asked to present his views to the society. This he did in 1911, and his ideas were denounced by the society. As a consequence, Adler resigned as its president, and a few months later severed his connection with Freudian psychoanalysis.

Adler then formed his own group, which became known as Individual Psychology and which attracted many followers. During the First World War, Adler served as a physician in the Austrian army, and after the war he became interested in child guidance and established the first guidance clinics in the Vienna school system.

In 1935 Adler settled in the United States, where he continued his practice as a psychiatrist and served as professor of medical psychology at the Long Island College of Medicine. Adler's ideas are disseminated in the United States by the American Society of Adlerian Psychology, with branches in New York, Chicago, and Los Angeles, and through its journal, *The American Journal of Individual Psychology.*

Adler's chief concept is that of the **creative self.** The creative power of the self organizes and determines the individual's personality by establishing what Adler called the **style of life.** Other important Adlerian concepts are **fictional finalism, striving for superiority, inferiority feelings, compensation,** and **social interest.**

CREATIVE SELF

The creative self is a personal, subjective system which interprets and makes meaningful the experiences of the individual. It searches for experiences and even creates experiences that will help the person to fulfill his unique **style of life.** The creative self gives the qualities of unity, consistency, and individuality to the personality. It is the active principle of human life.

STYLE OF LIFE

The style of life is a distinctive, unique conglomerate of motives, traits, interests, and values which exhibit themselves in every act a person performs. A person's style of life dictates what he will learn, how he will behave, how he will think, and what experiences will be incorporated into his personality. Experiences that are not pertinent to the style of life are ignored, rejected, or repressed.

The style of life of an individual is unique; no other person has an identical one. The style of life is developed and established by the creative self. It is formed early in childhood, by the age of four or five.

FICTIONAL FINALISM

Adler believed, unlike Freud, that man is motivated more by his expectations for the future than by experiences of the past. These future expectations may be purely fictional—that is, ideals which are not capable of being realized—yet they exercise a profound influence on a person's behavior. They spur him to greater and greater accomplishments. The normal person can, when necessity requires it, free himself from the influence of these fictions and face reality, something that the neurotic person is incapable of doing.

STRIVING FOR SUPERIORITY

The striving for superiority is a striving for the perfection of one's own development, not a desire to be superior to other people. This striving for superiority is inherent in every person, although each individual has his own way of trying to complete himself. Adler observes that the neurotic person strives for selfish goals, whereas the normal person strives for goals that are socially beneficial.

INFERIORITY FEELINGS

The *"inferiority complex,"* as it is often called, is one of the best-known Adlerian concepts. Feelings of inferiority arise from a sense of incompletion or imperfection in any sphere of a person's life. They cause one to strive to overcome the imperfection. This striving is what Adler calls **compensation.**

Compensation. Everyone is familiar with the example of a boy who is a weakling and turns himself into a strong, muscular man by exercising strenuously and regularly. He is said to be compensating for his physical inferiority. Compensation is merely another name for striving for superiority.

SOCIAL INTEREST

Social interest is an inborn characteristic of man that makes him want to contribute to society in order to make it more perfect. The individual tries to perfect in society that which cannot be perfected within himself. Social interest, Adler said, is the ultimate compensation for the inferiorities of individual human beings. Social interest causes a person to subordinate private gain to public welfare.

REFERENCES

Adler, A. *Practice and Theory of Individual Psychology.* New York: Harcourt, Brace, and World, 1927.

Adler, A. *The Science of Living.* New York: Greenberg, 1929.

Adler, A. *What Life Should Mean to You.* Boston: Little, Brown, 1931.

Adler, A. *Social Interest.* New York: Putnam, 1939.

Ansbacher, H. L., and R. R. Ansbacher, eds. *The Individual Psychology of Alfred Adler.* New York: Basic Books, 1956.

Ansbacher, H. L., and R. R. Ansbacher, eds. *Superiority and Social Interest by Alfred Adler.* Evanston, Ill.: Northwestern University Press, 1964.

Gordon W. Allport

1897–1967

Allport represented, perhaps better than any other contemporary theorist, the synthesis of traditional psychology, which studies general psychological processes, and the study of the individual personality. For Allport, each person is a unique organization of traits, dispositions, habits, attitudes, intentions, and motives. Allport was deeply influenced by William James (see p. 91), and resembled him in having a brilliant writing style, an eclectic orientation, an interest in the self, and a warm humanism.

Gordon Willard Allport, one of four sons of a physician, was born in Montezuma, Indiana, on November 11, 1897. He described his homelife as being characterized by plain Protestant piety and hard work. His mother, a former schoolteacher, encouraged the children in philosophical enquiries and stressed the importance of religion. His father operated a clinic in the home for many years and assigned the children responsibilities in assisting him.

After graduating from high school in Cleveland, Ohio, where his parents had moved, Allport followed his brother, Floyd, who also became a psychologist, to Harvard. Service in the First World War interrupted his education briefly. After receiving his A.B. degree in 1919, he took a teaching position at Robert College in Istanbul, Turkey, and then returned to Harvard, where he received his Ph.D. in psychology at the age of twenty-four. He then spent two years studying in Germany and England. Returning to the United States, he was for a year at Dartmouth College, and then joined the psychology department at Harvard, where he remained for the rest of his life. Allport died on October 9, 1967.

During his career, Allport received virtually every professional honor that psychologists have to offer. He was a prolific writer, but his two most important books are *Personality: A Psychological Interpretation* (1937), and a thorough revision of it 24 years later, entitled *Pattern and Growth in Personality* (1961).

Allport's chief concepts are those of **trait, personal disposition, proprium, functional autonomy,** and the **mature personality.**

TRAIT

In 1937 Allport had differentiated between traits that were common to a large number of people and traits that were unique to the individual. In 1961, common traits were simply called traits, and individual traits were called personal dispositions or morphogenic traits.

A trait is defined as a "neuropsychic structure having the capacity to render many stimuli functionally equivalent, and to initiate and guide equivalent (meaningfully consistent) forms of adaptive and expressive behavior" (1961, p. 347). "To render many stimuli functionally equivalent" means to react to different situations in the same way. For example, a person who is assertive tends to be assertive in many different situations. "To initiate and guide" means that a trait acts as a motive as well as being a form of behavior. A person who has the trait of assertiveness needs to express this trait.

PERSONAL DISPOSITION (MORPHOGENIC TRAIT)

A personal disposition is defined in the same way as a trait, except that the personal disposition is peculiar to the individual.

Allport identifies three classes of personal dispositions according to the degree of their generality in the personality. These are **cardinal, central,** and **secondary dispositions.**

Cardinal disposition. This is so general a disposition that almost every act of a person who possesses one appears traceable to its influence. Cardinal dispositions are rare, however, and are to be found in very few people.

Central disposition. A central disposition is one that is highly characteristic of the individual, is frequently called into action, and is very easy to identify. Allport suggests that the number of central dispositions by which a person can be fairly accurately known is surprisingly small, perhaps five to ten.

Secondary disposition. This type is more limited in its occurrence, less important in the description of the person, and more specific. A person may have a large number of secondary dispositions.

PROPRIUM

This is Allport's term for the functions that have been ascribed to the self. The proprium might also be called selfhood. The proprium is not inborn, but develops in time.

Allport identifies seven aspects of the proprium and their appearance in the development of the individual. During the first three years of childhood these three aspects appear: a sense of bodily self, a sense of continuing self-identity, and self-esteem or pride. Between the ages of four and six, two other aspects appear: the extension of self, and a self-image. Between six and twelve, the child acquires the self-awareness that he can deal with his problems by means of reason and thought. During adolescence, intentions, long range purposes, and distant goals emerge. These are called *propriate strivings.*

FUNCTIONAL AUTONOMY

This is Allport's most distinctive concept, for it embraces his theory of motivation. The concept simply states that a given form of behavior may become a goal in itself, in spite of the fact that it was originally engaged in for some other reason. A more formal definition formulated by Allport is as follows: "Functional autonomy regards adult motives as varied, and as self-sustaining contemporary systems, growing out of antecedent systems, but functionally independent of them" (1961, p. 227). For example, a child may be pressured into practicing playing the piano, but after a few months comes to enjoy it for its own sake. He likes to play the piano, and requires no other motivation beyond his enjoyment. The reason for practicing has become independent of any earlier reasons. Generally speaking, adult motives are for the most part different from those of the child. This means that the adult is relatively divorced from his past.

Allport recognizes two levels of functional autonomy, **perseverative** and **propriate.**

Perseverative functional autonomy applies to such repetitive acts as addictions, rituals, and routines. Drug addiction and alcoholism are familiar examples.

Propriate functional autonomy refers to acquired interests, values, sentiments, intentions, cardinal and central personal dispositions, self-image, and life style.

MATURE PERSONALITY

Allport is one of the few psychologists who has attempted to define the concept of the mature personality. The mature personality must possess an *extension of self.* He should be able to participate in and enjoy a wide variety of different activities. His satisfactions should be many and diverse, rather than few and stereotyped. Extension of self involves projection into the future—planning and hoping, for example. The mature individual must be able *to relate himself warmly to others* and be *emotionally secure* and *accepting of himself.* He should be *realistically oriented,* both with respect to himself and with respect to external reality. He should have *humor* and *insight.* Finally, the mature person has a unifying *philosophy of life.*

REFERENCES

Allport, G. W. *Personality: A Psychological Interpretation.* New York: Holt, 1937.

Allport, G. W. *The Nature of Personality: Selected Papers.* Cambridge, Mass.: Addison-Wesley, 1950.

Allport, G. W. *Pattern and Growth in Personality.* New York: Holt, Rinehart, and Winston, 1961.

Allport, G. W. *The Person in Psychology: Selected Essays.* Boston: Beacon, 1968.

Andras Angyal

1902–1960

Andras Angyal, like Kurt Goldstein (see p. 66), felt a need for a new science of personality that would not be primarily psychological, sociological, or physiological in character, but would embrace all aspects of a person as a whole. This new theory was called *organismic* or *holistic* theory. Unlike Goldstein, however, Angyal believed that it is impossible to differentiate the organism from the environment. He insisted that the interpenetration of the organism and the environment is so complex that they cannot be unraveled; to do so would destroy the natural unity of the whole, and create an artificial distinction between organism and environment.

Andras Angyal was born in Hungary in 1902, and was educated at the University of Vienna, where he received his Ph.D. in 1927. He then attended the University of Turin in Italy to study medicine, receiving his M.D. in 1932. That same year he came to the United States as a Rockefeller fellow in the Department of Anthropology at Yale University. He was actively engaged in research at Worcester State Hospital, Massachusetts, for a number of years, and served as Director of Research there from 1937 to 1945. He left that position to enter private psychiatric practice in Boston. In 1953 Angyal became a psychiatric consultant at the Counseling Center of Brandeis University. He died in 1960. He is known primarily for his book *Foundations for a Science of Personality* (1941).

Angyal's unique concept is that of the **biosphere,** which encloses the organism and the environment in an inseparable entity. The most basic division that can be made in the biosphere is that between the organismic pole, which is called the **subject,** and the environmental pole, which is called the **object.** The holistic units of the biosphere are called **systems.** The energy of the biosphere is supplied by tensions that arise between the environmental pole and the organismic pole of the biosphere. These opposing directional trends of the organism and the environment within the biosphere are called **autonomy** and **homonomy,** respectively. There are three main dimensions within the biosphere: **vertical, progressive,** and **transverse.** The organism is capable of developing ideas about itself; these self-conceptions constitute the **symbolic self.**

BIOSPHERE

The biosphere is a holistic entity which includes both the individual and the environment "not as interacting parts, not as constituents which have independent existence, but as aspects of a single reality which can be separated only by abstraction" (1941, p. 100). Although the biosphere is an indivisible unit, it is possible to distinguish processes that are more organismic from those that are more environmental. However, processes can never be exclusively one or the other; they are always biospheric.

Subject. The most basic division of the biosphere is that of subject and object. The subject is the organism and constitutes one pole of the biosphere.

Object. The object is the environment, and constitutes the other pole of the biosphere. Neither organismic processes nor environmental events alone reflect reality; rather, *biospheric occurrences,* which are bipolar in character, are the reality of personality. The whole dynamics of life consist of the interactions between the two poles of the biosphere.

Systems. Angyal calls the holistic units of the biosphere systems because of their complexity. A system may include as many components as are necessary to explain a given phenomenon. The components of a system are connected with one another by virtue of their respective positions in the system. Systems can be either rigid or plastic. A rigid system has fixed immovable positions for its parts, whereas in a plastic system the parts can move around and form new connections.

Autonomy. The trend toward autonomy consists of the expansion of the organismic pole of the biosphere by assimilating and mastering the environment. The trend toward autonomy is expressed by means of various specific channels, for instance, by desires for superiority, for acquisition, for exploration, and for achievement. Angyal has also called autonomy *self-determination.*

Homonomy. The trend toward homonomy motivates the person to fit himself to the environment and to participate in something that is larger than his individual self. He tries to form a harmonious union with the social group, with nature, or with an omnipotent being. Angyal has also called this trend *self-surrender.*

Self-expansion. Although autonomy or self-determination and homonomy or self-surrender may appear to be opposed to one another, they are really two phases of a more inclusive trend of the biosphere, that of self-expansion. By enlarging both poles, the whole biosphere is thereby expanded.

Vertical Dimension. This dimension extends from overt behavior at the surface of the biosphere down to underlying attitudes at the core of the biosphere. Aggression, for example, is the overt expression of an underlying hostility which can be traced to even deeper-lying attitudes. The goal of surface behavior is to create biospheric conditions which represent the satisfaction of a need within the personality.

Progressive Dimension. This dimension consists of a series of acts which brings a person toward a final goal, step by step.

Transverse dimension. This dimension consists of the coordination of discrete acts into a larger, better integrated, and more effective behavior unit.

Symbolic self. Man is capable of developing ideas about himself as an organism because many of his organic processes become conscious. The sum total of these self-conceptions constitutes his symbolic self. However, the symbolic self is not always a reliable representation of the organism, so that if a person's behavior is governed by the symbolic self, his actions may not be appropriate to the real needs of the organism.

REFERENCES

Angyal, A. *Foundations for a Science of Personality.* New York: Commonwealth Fund, 1941.

Angyal, A. *Neurosis and Treatment: A Holistic Theory.* New York: Wiley, 1965.

Albert Bandura

b. 1925

What determines what a child will learn and how he will behave? A popular answer to this question is that the child learns by observing his parents and older children, and by imitating their behavior. Despite its popular appeal, the concept of imitation was not accorded much status by psychologists until fairly recently. With the appearance of Neal Miller's and John Dollard's *Social Learning and Imitation* in 1941, imitation or modeling, as it is also called, began to gain respectability. The person who has been chiefly responsible for establishing the concept on a solid empirical foundation is the Stanford psychologist, Albert Bandura.

Albert Bandura was born in Canada on December 4, 1925, and earned his B.A. in 1949 at the University of British Columbia. His M.A. and Ph.D. (1952) were obtained at the University of

Iowa. Since 1953, he has been a member of the psychology faculty at Stanford University.

Bandura is a social learning theorist and researcher in the tradition of Clark Hull (see p. 85) and Hull's students, Kenneth Spence and Robert Sears, with whom he studied at Iowa. Bandura is well-known for his work on aggressive behavior and on the role of **modeling** or **imitation** in learning. His research is especially concerned with the acquisition and modification of personality traits in children.

IMITATION (MODELING)

A simple illustration of imitative behavior is the following. When I am with a person who begins to yawn, I find myself yawning, too. This echoing of behavior is supposed to be responsible not only for the socialization of the child, but also for fads and fashions, mass hysteria, the bandwagon effect, and many other forms of social contagion.

Bandura and his associates have expanded the concept of imitation or modeling in many important ways. For instance, in the foregoing example of yawning, yawning is already something a person can do. Imitation, in this instance, is merely a matter of matching behaviors that are already in existence. Bandura has shown we can learn *new* behavior by observing another person performing an act. We do not even have to perform the act which we are watching the model perform in order to be able to do it at a later time. For example, a child may watch a television show and later act out some of the things he saw on the screen. Moreover, imitation can occur even though neither the model nor the observer is being rewarded for performing the act. This means that learning by observation or imitation differs from Pavlov's classical conditioning (see p. 135) and from Skinner's operant reinforcement (see p. 156).

Although reward and punishment are not essential for learning by imitation, they can have an influence, as Bandura has demonstrated. A child is more likely to imitate a model who is being rewarded for his acts and less likely to imitate a model who is being punished. This means that a person does not have to be rewarded or punished himself, but can have his behavior modified merely by observing another person being rewarded or punished. This is called **vicarious learning.**

Vicarious learning. The word vicarious means experiencing the same feeling or emotion that another person is displaying. Movies are said to be a source of vicarious pleasures and sufferings for the spectator. Bandura has shown that a person who watches the emotional reactions of a model to a stimulus not only experiences the same emotion, but also tends to become emotionally conditioned to the stimulus that is causing the model's reaction. Subsequently, when the stimulus is presented in the absence of the model, the subject reacts emotionally to it. Many fears and hostilities are acquired in this way.

REFERENCES

Bandura, A. *Principles of Behavior Modification.* New York: Holt, Rinehart, and Winston, 1969.

Bandura, A., ed. *Psychological Modeling: Conflicting Theories.* Chicago: Aldine-Atherton, 1971.

Bandura, A. *Aggression: A Social Learning Analysis.* Englewood Cliffs, N.J.: Prentice-Hall, 1973.

Bandura, A., and R. H. Walters. *Adolescent Aggression.* New York: Ronald Press, 1959.

Bandura, A., and R. H. Walters. *Social Learning and Personality Development.* New York: Holt, Rinehart, and Winston, 1963.

Miller, N. E., and J. Dollard. *Social Learning and Imitation.* New Haven: Yale University Press, 1941.

Medard Boss

b. 1903

Medard Boss is a leading exponent of existential psychology. Existential psychology is an offshoot of the existential movement in philosophy, which rose to prominence following the Second World War. Some of the names associated with the movement are Jean Paul Sartre and Albert Camus in France, Martin Heidegger and Karl Jaspers in Germany, Ludwig Binswanger in Switzerland, R. D. Laing in England, and Rollo May and Adrian Van Kaam in the United States. It influenced the thinking of such American psychologists as Carl Rogers (see p. 147) and Abraham Maslow (see p. 116).

Existential psychology may be defined as an empirical science of human existence which employs the method of phenomenological analysis. By phenomenological analysis is meant the description of the contents of immediate awareness, what is going on in a person's mind right now. The basic tenet of existential psychology is that man is free to be what he wants to be; therefore, he alone is responsible for his own existence.

Medard Boss was born in St. Gallen, Switzerland, on October 4, 1903. When he was two years old, his parents moved to Zurich, where Boss has resided ever since. After trying unsuccessfully to become an artist, Boss decided to study medicine. He received his medical degree from the University of Zurich in 1928. Prior to obtaining the degree, he studied in Paris and Vienna and was analyzed by Sigmund Freud. From 1928 to 1932, Boss was assistant to Eugen Bleuler, the famous director of the Burgholzli psychiatric hospital in Zurich. Thereafter, for two years, Boss underwent further psychoanalytic training in London and Germany with such prominent psychoanalysts as Ernest Jones, Karen Horney (see p. 81), Otto Fenichel, Hanns Sachs, and Wilhelm Reich. While in Germany he also worked with Kurt Goldstein (see p. 66). After this excellent preparation, Boss went into private practice as a psychoanalyst at the age of 32. About this time, he and several other psychotherapists began a series of monthly meetings at the home of Carl Jung (see p. 95).

The year 1946 was a turning point in Boss's intellectual life. It was then that he became personally acquainted with the leading German existential philosopher, Martin Heidegger. As a result of their close and continuing association, Boss generated an existential form of psychotherapy which he called *Daseinsanalysis*. Boss's outlook was also greatly influenced by his encounter with the wisdom of India in two trips he made there in 1956 and 1958. He described his experiences in a book, *A Psychiatrist Discovers India* (1965).

For a number of years, Boss was president of the International Federation for Medical Psychotherapy and is now its honorary president. Since 1954, he has been professor of psychotherapy at the University of Zurich. In 1971, he became scientific director of the Daseinsanalytic Institute of Psychotherapy and Psychosomatics. In the same year, he was the recipient of the "Great Therapist Award" given by the American Psychiatric Association. Boss has lectured at universities in the United States, and some of his books have been translated into English. The most important one is *Psychoanalysis and Daseinsanalysis* (1963).

Boss calls his method of existential psychotherapy *Daseins-analysis. Dasein* is a German word which has been translated into English by the hyphenated expression being-in-the-world. Being-in-the-world or *Dasein* constitutes the whole of man's existence; hence the name existential psychology. Daseinsanalysis requires the careful elucidation of the specific nature of the individual's existence, his way of **being-in-the-world.**

BEING-IN-THE-WORLD

This is the basic concept of existential psychology. It expresses the idea that the world and the individual are a oneness. The individual has no existence apart from the world, and the world has no existence apart from the individual. Neither one can exist alone, nor are they to be conceived as separate but interacting entities.

The world is disclosed in the individual, and the individual discloses the world. These disclosures constitute the phenomena of existence. Nothing lies behind these phenomena; they are neither cause nor effect, nor are they subject and object. They are the whole reality of human existence.

Existential psychology as an empirical science consists of describing these phenomena as fully and as accurately as possible. In so doing, it does not employ a technical vocabulary. It uses the words that best describe the phenomena. Often, these are commonplace, everyday words. Sometimes, the vocabulary is quite poetic.

There are two primary dimensions of being-in-the-world. These are **spatiality** and **temporality.**

Spatiality refers to the closeness or remoteness with which a person is in-the-world. The distance between himself and other persons or objects is one of degree, from very close to very remote.

Temporality refers to the unfolding of the world. This unfolding takes place in time, so that a person always has a past, a present, and a future. Human existence is primarily a historical event. Man is the totality of all of his past, present, and future **possibilities** of relating to the world.

POSSIBILITIES

Man carries within himself an almost infinite number of possibilities for disclosing the world. He is responsible for using these possibilities to the fullest extent. When he accepts this responsibility, he is then exercising his freedom as a man. "Man's freedom consists in becoming ready for accepting and letting be all that is" (Boss, 1963, p. 48). When an individual fails to carry out the mandate to realize all his possibilities, he experiences a sense of **guilt.**

GUILT

Guilt is a primary and persistent fact of human existence. It cannot be avoided or overcome, because the individual is always in debt to the myriad possibilities for disclosing the world. Every choice means that all the other possibilities are rejected. It is this failure to realize all his possibilities that makes a person feel guilty.

In addition to guilt, there are other limitations on man's freedom. The most important of these limitations are **constriction** and **mood.**

CONSTRICTION

Imagine a person whose whole existence, or a large portion of it, is absorbed by a single preoccupation. It may be making money, seeking fame, eating, drinking, or acquiring possessions. Such a person leads an impoverished, constricted life. He is enslaved by his compulsion.

MOOD

At any particular time, how a person will act may be determined by his mood of the moment. If he is anxious and insecure, his being-in-the-world will be attuned to threats and dangers. The mood of hunger attunes him to a world of eatables. Long-lasting moods narrow one's openness to the world.

NOTHINGNESS

Nothingness is the presence within human existence of nonexistence. To fall into nothingness is to lose one's being, to become nothing. The extent to which the possibilities of existence fall short of fulfillment is the extent to which nonbeing has taken over being. Dread of nothingness is a recurrent topic in the literature of existentialism.

BECOMING

This is the most important developmental concept of existential psychology. Existence is never static; it is always in the process of becoming something new, of transcending itself. The goal of existence is to become completely human, that is, to fulfill or actualize as many ways of being-in-the-world as is humanly possible. To fail to do this means that the person remains undeveloped and stunted.

REFERENCES

Boss, M. *The Analysis of Dreams.* New York: Philosophical Library, 1958.
Boss, M. *Psychoanalysis and Daseinsanalysis.* New York: Basic Books, 1963.
Boss, M. *A Psychiatrist Discovers India.* London: Oswald Wolff, 1965.

Egon Brunswik

1903–1955

Most people would probably agree that we live in a world of considerable flux and change. Even the same object is rarely seen from exactly the same perspective on different occasions—a fact that the cubist painters exploited. Despite the inconstancy of the environment as well as the inconstancy of the body, we manage to impose a fair amount of order and constancy on a changing environment. How is this accomplished? One answer is to be found in Egon Brunswik's concept of **probabilistic functionalism.**

Egon Brunswik was born in Budapest, Hungary, on March 18, 1903. He attended a technical school for two years, intending to become an engineer. However, an interest in psychology caused him to transfer to the University of Vienna, which awarded him a Ph.D. in 1927. His association with the University of Vienna continued until 1935. During these years, he came under the influence of the famous Vienna circle of *logical positivism.* Logical positivism maintains that statements which are not based on observable data are meaningless. It also believes that concepts should be defined in terms of the operations which are performed in observing or measuring them. Finally, it believes in the unity of all sciences. Brunswik's writings and research reflect the influence of these ideas.

In 1935, Brunswik and his psychologist wife, Else Frenkel-Brunswik, went to the University of California, Berkeley, upon the invitation of Edward Tolman (see p. 172) and remained there until Brunswik's death on July 7, 1955.

Brunswik's concept of probabilistic functionalism addresses itself to the question of how an organism can function and achieve its aims in a probabilistic or uncertain environment.

PROBABILISTIC FUNCTIONALISM

Brunswik points out that there are three kinds of events, plus the relationships that exist among them, in which psychologists are interested. These are **central, proximal,** and **distal events.**

Central events are those that take place within the organism.

Proximal events are those that take place at the boundaries of the organism. They consist of stimuli, sensory processes, bodily movements, and acts.

Distal events are those with which the individual is not in direct contact. They are such things as objects, past events, present achievements, and plans for the future.

Correspondences between central and proximal events, and between proximal and distal events, are not exact. Consequently, in order for the individual to adjust correctly to distal events, it is often necessary for him to make guesses, on the basis of proximal information, about what the environment "out there" is like. These guesses are combined, weighed, and acted upon according to their assumed probabilities of being correct.

Suppose you are walking down the street and see a person walking ahead of you who looks familiar. You think it may be your friend, Mr. A, but you are not sure. What you do, according to the concept of probabilistic functionalism, is to accumulate, combine, and weigh the proximal cues you are receiving from the distal person, and then decide on the basis of this information whether it is or is not Mr. A. The correctness of your guess is determined, of course, by overtaking the person in question; on the basis of the additional information you obtain when looking at him face to face, you confirm or fail to confirm your guess.

Not all discriminations are this chancy, however. In fact, it is astonishing how many of our perceptions, discriminations, and actions are absolutely correct despite the probabilistic nature of the environment.

For making studies of probabilistic functionalism, Brunswik proposed a new methodology which he called **representative design.**

REPRESENTATIVE DESIGN

Laboratory experiments in psychology often employ the method of allowing one condition to vary while holding all the other conditions constant. One is thereby able to determine what effect, if any, the varying condition has on behavior. Brunswik believes that the controlled experiment performed in the laboratory is often artificial and yields superficial results. Brunswik suggests that psychologists should study a particular form of behavior in which they are interested as it expresses itself in a representative sample of natural, nonlaboratory situations. This method of representative design, Brunswik believes, would yield more useful knowledge of man's behavior in the everyday world than the single-variable, controlled laboratory experiment does.

REFERENCES

Brunswik, E. *The Conceptual Framework of Psychology.* Chicago: University of Chicago Press, 1952.

Brunswik, E. *Perception and the Representative Design of Psychological Experiments.* Berkeley, Calif.: University of California Press, 1956.

Hammond, K. R. *The Psychology of Egon Brunswik.* New York: Holt, Rinehart, and Winston, 1966.

Postman, L., and E. C. Tolman. "Brunswik's probabilistic functionalism." In S. Koch, ed., *Psychology: A Study of a Science* (New York: McGraw-Hill, 1959), I, 502–564.

Raymond B. Cattell

b. 1905

Cattell's concepts grew out of his investigations using the method of *multivariate design.* This method, as the word multivariate suggests, consists of measuring the behaviors of a person or a group of persons in many different test situations. The resulting measured variables—they are often paper-and-pencil test scores, but they also include behavior ratings, questionnaires, and physiological measures—are then subjected to a form of statistical analysis known as factor analysis. Factor analysis produces a set of factors or, in Cattell's terminology, **traits.** Knowing a person's trait structure, one can then make predictions about how he will behave in any specific situation.

Raymond Bernard Cattell was born in Staffordshire, England, on March 20, 1905, and received all his education in England. He majored in chemistry as an undergraduate at the University of London and then changed to psychology for his graduate work.

He studied under Charles Spearman, the father of the factor analysis method, and was awarded the Ph.D. in 1929 by the University of London. From 1928 to 1937, Cattell was a college teacher and director of a psychological clinic. For his contributions to personality research, the University of London conferred the Doctor of Science degree on him in 1937. At this time, Cattell came to the United States, worked with E. L. Thorndike (see p. 168) for a year, became professor of psychology at Clark University in Massachusetts, and served as a lecturer at Harvard University. In 1944 he accepted a position as research professor of psychology and director of the Laboratory of Personality and Group Analysis at the University of Illinois, where he has remained.

Cattell, with the assistance of many associates and graduate students, has been an indefatigable researcher and a prolific writer. His books, monographs, and articles number in the hundreds, rivaling the productivity of Jean Piaget (see p. 139). Cattell has also devised a number of psychological tests which are widely used for research purposes and in clinical, school, and work settings.

Cattell's most important concept is that of **trait.** Personality is viewed by him as a structure of traits, and he has identified different classes of traits that make up this structure. These include **surface** and **source traits, environmental-mold** and **constitutional traits, ability** and **temperamental traits,** and **dynamic traits.** He has also proposed a concept, **syntality,** which refers to the traits that are characteristic of a group of people.

TRAIT

A trait is a durable mental structure that is inferred from observed behavior. It accounts for the regularity and consistency of behavior. The meaning of this concept will become clearer as we discuss the various classes of traits.

Surface traits. A surface trait represents a cluster of similar overt behaviors. For example, when a person acts aggressively in a number of different situations, he is said to manifest the trait of aggression. Surface traits can be observed directly.

Source traits are those traits which underlie and produce surface traits. For example, intelligence can be regarded as a source trait because it partly determines several surface traits. There are fewer source traits, and they are much more important than surface traits. Source traits are identified by using the method of factor analysis.

Environmental-mold traits result primarily from environmental influences.

Constitutional traits result from internal, physiological conditions, some of which are hereditary in character.

Ability traits are those that determine the effectiveness of a person in dealing with problems and tasks. Scholastic ability, manual dexterity, and artistic talent are examples of ability traits.

Temperament traits include such characteristics as emotionality, energy level, speed, impulsiveness, dominance, sensitivity, and self-assurance.

Dynamic traits are motivational in character. They arouse a person to act, and they direct his actions toward a goal. There are three kinds of dynamic traits: **attitudes, ergs,** and **sentiments.**

Attitudes. An attitude is an interest of a certain intensity in some course of action with respect to some object, person, or idea. The statement "I desperately want to get into graduate school" indicates an intensity of interest ("desperately"), and a course of action ("get into") toward an object ("graduate school").

Ergs. An erg is an inborn disposition to pay attention to a certain class of objects, to experience a specific emotion in regard to them, and to initiate a course of action which leads to a goal. Ergs are the basic driving forces in the personality. Examples of ergs are sex, gregariousness, parental protectiveness, curiosity, fear, and self-assertion. The concept of erg is virtually the same as McDougall's instinct (see p. 119).

Sentiments. A sentiment is the same as an erg except that sentiments are acquired rather than inborn. Sentiments are organized around significant persons in one's life (mother, father, spouse, offspring), activities (vocation, hobbies, sports), institutions (nation, religion, school), and most importantly one's self, which Cattell regards as the master sentiment.

SYNTALITY

This concept recognizes the fact that a group can have a characteristic trait structure. Syntality is to a group what personality is to an individual. Thus, families, schools, occupations, religions, and nations all have their own cluster of traits. It is important to study syntality, because the traits of a group directly shape the personality of a member of the group. The syntality of an individual's own family is probably the chief molding influence on his personality.

REFERENCES

Cattell, R. B. *Description and Measurement of Personality.* New York: World, 1946.

Cattell, R. B. *Personality: A Systematic, Theoretical, and Factual Study.* New York: McGraw-Hill, 1950.

Cattell, R. B. *Personality and Motivation, Structure and Measurement.* New York: Harcourt, Brace, and World, 1957.

Cattell, R. B., ed. *Handbook of Multivariate Experimental Psychology.* Chicago: Rand, McNally, 1966.

Cattell, R. B. *Personality and Mood by Questionnaire.* San Francisco: Jossey-Bass, 1973.

Erik H. Erikson

b. 1902

One of Freud's basic ideas is expressed by the saying "The child is father of the man." He believed that the character of the adult is largely determined by the experiences one has during childhood. Erikson's chief contribution to psychoanalytic theory consisted of describing the sequence of developmental phases an individual passes through from infancy to adulthood and identifying the conflicts or problems associated with each phase.

Erik Homburger Erikson was born on June 15, 1902, near Frankfurt, Germany, of Danish parents. His parents separated shortly before their son was born, and his mother married Dr. Homburger, a German physician of Karlsruhe, where young Erik attended school. Upon completing high school, Erikson spent a year wandering through Europe, trying to find out what direction his life should take. He finally decided to become an artist and to teach art. After several years of training in art, Erikson accepted an invitation to teach in a small private school in Vienna, one of whose founders was Anna Freud, the daughter of Sigmund Freud. Erikson became well acquainted with the Freud family and began analysis with Anna Freud. Through her encouragement, Erikson began to study psychoanalysis at the Vienna Psychoanalytic Society. He also studied the Montessori method of education, which stresses the development of the whole child.

Shortly after graduating from the Vienna Psychoanalytic Society in 1933, Erikson and his family departed for the United States, where he became the first child psychoanalyst in Boston. He also held positions at the Harvard Medical School and the Massachusetts General Hospital, and worked with Henry Murray (see p. 127) at the Harvard Psychological Clinic. After three years in Boston, Erikson accepted a position at the Yale University Institute of Human Relations and an instructorship in the Yale Medical School. Offered an opportunity to observe Sioux Indian children in South Dakota, Erikson left Yale to live on a Sioux reservation. At the end of the year, he went to Berkeley and became associated with the Institute of Child Welfare of the University of California. While in California, Erikson studied the Yurok Indians. After ten years of observing children in various settings, Erikson published his findings in a very influential book, *Childhood and Society* (1963). He then left California to take a position at the Austen Riggs Center in Massachusetts, a prominent psychiatric center. Erikson's career finally came full circle when he returned to Harvard University as a professor of human development. He retired in 1970.

Erikson is known throughout the world for his work and publications. He was awarded both the Pulitzer Prize and the National Book Award for his writings. Erikson also made important contributions in the area of psychobiography and psychohistory with the publication of *Young Man Luther* (1958) and *Gandhi's Truth* (1969).

Erikson's principal concepts are those of **epigenesis,** the **life cycle,** and the search for **identity.**

EPIGENESIS

Epigenesis refers to growth or development. As Erikson sees it, epigenesis consists of a sequence of developmental stages in which a certain part of the personality becomes ascendant at each stage. The individual must pass through all these stages before he can acquire a sense of his own identity.

Given the epigenetic principle as a general statement of growth, Erikson then spells out the actual stages through which the individual passes. This is called the **life cycle.**

LIFE CYCLE

Erikson identifies five stages between birth and adolescence. During infancy, the first stage, the baby experiences a *mutuality of recognition* with the mother. This mutuality is the basis for an emergence of a feeling of *trust* in the infant. Lacking trust, the baby would be severely handicapped in the following stages. It is, therefore, an immensely important period.

When the child has trust in his environment, he can then proceed to develop independence and a sense of his own *autonomy.* This normally occurs during early childhood.

Later in childhood but before he enters school, the child acquires *initiative.* He learns to do things for himself without being told, and he begins to practice various roles which he will have to play later in life. During the early school years, the fourth stage in the life cycle, the child learns how to work and to be *industrious.* He identifies with the tasks that he has to do.

The development of a sense of trust, autonomy, initiative, and industry are necessary antecedents for the very crucial period of adolescence, during which one acquires an **identity.**

IDENTITY

During adolescence, the individual experiences a sense of his own identity as a unique human being. He learns that he has his own inherent characteristics, his own preferences, and his own aspirations, and that he has control over his own life. It is a time of defining what he is and what he wants to be.

The activating agent in identity formation is the ego or the conscious self. When the adolescent acquires what Erikson calls *ego identity,* he can then proceed to form his own identity. An ego that possesses its own identity, instead of being identified with others, recognizes what talents, aptitudes, and skills, what identifications with other people and with the environment, what defenses against threats and anxiety, and what impulses, needs, and roles are most appropriate and effective for the individual. All these ego-selected characteristics are assembled and integrated by the ego to form one's identity.

IDENTITY CRISIS

Every new stage of the life cycle constitutes a potential hazard because each stage is a crucial turning point in the individual's development. If conditions are unfavorable for the development of trust, it will be difficult for the child to become autonomous, and if he does not become autonomous, it will be difficult for him to acquire initiative. Without initiative, he cannot become industrious.

By far the most serious crisis a person faces occurs during identity formation. It is serious because failure to deal with the crisis successfully has far-reaching consequences. A person without a well-formed identity will encounter one problem after another during his adult life. Erikson points out that an identity crisis can occur at any time; it is not restricted to the adolescent period.

IDENTITY CONFUSION

The adolescent during the stage of identity formation is likely to suffer more deeply than ever before or ever again from a confusion of roles, or what Erikson calls **identity confusion.** This state causes the adolescent to feel isolated, empty, anxious, and indecisive. He feels he must make important decisions, but he is unable to do so. He also feels that society is pushing him to make decisions, and he becomes resistant.

During identity confusion, the adolescent may feel that he is regressing rather than progressing, and, in fact, a retreat to childhood appears to be a pleasant alternative to the complex involvement with an adult society. His behavior is very inconsistent and unpredictable during this chaotic state. At one moment he has an inner reservation not to commit himself to anyone in fear of being rejected, disappointed, or misled. The very next moment he may want to be a follower, lover, or disciple, no matter what the consequences of such a commitment may be.

REFERENCES

Coles, R. *Erik H. Erikson; The Growth of His Work.* Boston: Atlantic, Little, Brown, 1970.

Erikson, E. H. "Identity and the life cycle." In *Psychological Issues* (New York: International Universities Press, 1959), I, 1–171.

Erikson, E. H. *Childhood and Society.* New York: Norton, 2d ed., 1963.

Erikson, E. H. *Identity, Youth, and Crisis.* New York: Norton, 1968.

Leon Festinger

b. 1919

In 1957, a book entitled *A Theory of Cognitive Dissonance* by Leon Festinger, then a professor of psychology at Stanford University, was published. No recent concept in social psychology has stimulated more research than that of cognitive dissonance.

Leon Festinger was born in New York City on May 8, 1919. After completing his undergraduate education at the City College of New York in 1939, he went to the State University of Iowa, where he received an M.A. in 1940 and a Ph.D. in 1942. After teaching and doing research at various universities, including Iowa, Rochester, Massachusetts Institute of Technology, Michigan, and Minnesota, he became professor of psychology at Stanford University in 1955. In 1968, he joined the faculty of the New School for Social Research in New York City. Festinger views man as essentially a thinking individual who tries to bring order and coherence into his life.

Imagine the following situation. Two adult male friends, Mr. A and Mr. B, are arguing about the conduct of the "younger generation." Mr. A maintains that they are a pretty bad lot, irresponsible, undisciplined, unkempt, and indolent. Mr. B believes they are no worse than young people of previous generations, and in some respects they are even better. This lack of agreement is what Festinger labels **cognitive dissonance.**

COGNITIVE DISSONANCE

When two opinions, ideas, or beliefs are not in agreement, there is said to exist a condition of cognitive dissonance. Dissonance may exist between two people, as in the foregoing example, or it may also exist within the same person who holds conflicting views about something.

Dissonance is regarded by Festinger as being an uncomfortable condition to be in, so that efforts are made to reach *consonance* (agreement) or a state of harmony, and to avoid situations that might arouse dissonance. In other words, dissonance is a motive.

How is dissonance reduced? Consider the two men arguing about the younger generation. They will try to convince each other by giving evidence for their respective positions. It may turn out that each man will modify his original opinion, so that they finally reach a compromise which is agreeable to each of them. Or they may agree to disagree, and drop the argument. Or they may dissolve their friendship because the dissonance is too uncomfortable.

The concept of dissonance can be applied to any situation, not just social ones, in which a person is in disequilibrium (disharmony) with his environment or with himself, and attempts to return to equilibrium by thought and reason.

REFERENCE

Festinger, L. *A Theory of Cognitive Dissonance.* Evanston, Ill.: Row, Peterson, 1957.

Sigmund Freud
1856–1939

There is general agreement today that a science does not reach maturity by the steady accumulation of facts, concepts, laws, and hypotheses. Instead of this linear view, the history of a science is now regarded as one of the periodic revolutions in thought that drastically change the conceptual foundations of the science. One need only think of the impact of Copernicus, Newton, Darwin, Mendel, and Einstein. Psychology, too, has had its revolutions: behaviorism, which was initiated by Pavlov (see p. 135) and Watson (see p. 177); Gestalt psychology (see p. 57); and psychoanalysis, which was started by a Viennese psychiatrist, Sigmund Freud. Psychoanalysis, it is true, began as a method of treating mental patients, but it soon became a wholly new conception of man. The central hypothesis of psychoanalysis is that human behavior is determined in large part by unconscious motives. Freud is regarded as the explorer and mapper of the unconscious.

The founder of psychoanalysis, Sigmund Freud, was born in a small Czech town in Moravia near the Polish border on May 6, 1856, and died in London on September 23, 1939. For nearly eighty years, however, he resided in Vienna, and left that city only when the Nazis overran Austria. His father was a wool merchant. Freud was the first-born of eight children by his father's second wife. There were two sons, twenty odd years older than Freud, by his father's first wife. The family moved to Vienna when Freud was four.

Freud entered the world-famous medical school of the University of Vienna in 1873 with the intention of becoming a scientist and professor, not a practicing physician. His appetite for science was sharpened by his professor, Ernst Brücke, one of the very influential leaders of the Helmholtz school of medicine, which held that physiological processes are physiochemical in nature. But the limited opportunities for academic advancement for a Jew and the pressing needs of a growing family—Freud had six children—required him to enter private practice as a psychiatrist. In order to improve his skills, Freud studied for a year with the great French psychiatrist, Jean Charcot, who employed hypnotism for treating patients with nervous disorders, especially hysteria. Freud tried hypnotism with his patients, but he was not impressed with its efficacy. Much more effective, he discovered, was the talking-out or free-association method used by a Viennese colleague, Joseph Breuer, to ferret out the origins of neurotic symptoms. Freud collaborated with Breuer for several years and they wrote a book together, *Studies in Hysteria* (1895), but their relationship ended when Breuer refused to accept Freud's emphasis on sexual conflicts as the cause of hysteria.

Thereafter, Freud worked pretty much alone, developing the ideas which were to form the foundation of psychoanalytic theory and which culminated in the publication of his first great work, *The Interpretation of Dreams* (1900). Other books and articles, as well as lectures he gave at the University—Freud did succeed in becoming a professor after all—brought his theories and methods to the attention of physicians and scientists throughout the world, and soon he had a number of disciples, including Carl Jung (see p. 95) and Alfred Adler (see p. 7). It should also be noted that Freud's views were bitterly assailed.

Freud's first recognition by academic psychology came in 1909, when he was invited by the American psychologist G. Stanley Hall to give a series of lectures at Clark University in Worcester, Massachusetts. Freud's impact on psychology was not felt until the 1930's, however. The International Psychoanalytic Association was founded in 1910, and training institutes for psychoanalysis were established in many countries. Psychoanalysis became a world-wide movement, and Freud's name a household word.

Despite the pressures of organizational work and writing—his collected works fill twenty-three volumes—Freud continued to put in a full working day, seeing patients throughout his life. These patients provided him with data for his theoretical formulations, which were constantly being revised and elaborated. Another important source of information for Freud was the material he dredged up from his own unconscious. He began to analyze himself in 1897 and continued doing so until the end of his life, reserving the last half-hour of each day for this activity.

Freud's extensive writings embrace many different subjects: the techniques of psychoanalysis; illustrative case studies; the applications of psychoanalysis to the social sciences, history, biography, religion, and literature; as well as purely theoretical issues and broad surveys of psychoanalysis. Whatever the subject, Freud's style is elegant, exciting, and picturesque. He was well-acquainted with the classics of literature.

Freud was a very courageous man. He remained calm in the face of bitter and often very personal attacks. He refused to leave Vienna when the Nazis came to power until his friends persuaded him to do so for the safety of his family. His courage was severely tested by repeated operations on his jaw and mouth for cancer, from which he suffered for the last 16 years of his life and which was the cause of his death at the age of 83.

The concepts of Freud's theory of personality may be treated under three headings: structural, dynamic, and developmental. The principal structural concepts are **id, ego,** and **superego.** The principal dynamic concepts are **instinct, libido, cathexis, anti-cathexis,** and **anxiety.** The principal developmental concepts are **identificaction, displacement, defense mechanisms,** and **psycho-sexual stages.**

ID

The id (Latin for "it") consists of everything psychological that is inherited and that is present at birth, including the instincts. It is the reservoir of psychic energy which supplies the power for all psychological functioning. The contents and processes of the id are completely unconscious. The operations of the id are governed by the **pleasure principle** and the **primary process.**

Pleasure principle. When an uncomfortable level of undischarged energy (tension) is reached, the id automatically seeks to discharge the tension and return to a comfortably low level of energy. This principle of tension reduction by which the id operates is called the pleasure principle. In order to accomplish its aim of avoiding painful tension and obtaining pleasure, the id utilizes the **primary process.**

Primary process. The primary process attempts to discharge tension by forming an image of an object that will discharge the tension. For example, a hungry person has a mental image of food. In dreams, images of things we want appear to us. This is also called *wish-fulfillment.* Obviously, the primary process is not capable of reducing much tension. A hungry person cannot eat mental pictures of food. As a consequence, a new structure develops out of the id. This is called the **ego.**

EGO

The ego comes into existence because the needs of the organism require appropriate transactions with the outside world. A hungry person has to seek, find, and eat food before the tension of hunger can be eliminated.

The ego is the executive of the personality, because it controls the gateways to action, selects the features of the environment to which it will respond, and decides which needs will be satisfied and in what order. It has to try to integrate the conflicting demands of the id, the superego, and the external world.

The ego obeys the **reality principle,** and operates by means of the **secondary process** and **reality testing.**

Reality principle. The aim of the reality principle, in contrast to that of the pleasure principle, is to prevent the discharge of tension until an object which is appropriate for the satisfaction of the need has been discovered.

Secondary process. Whereas the primary process produces fantasies and hallucinations, the secondary process is one of realistic thinking. The higher intellectual functions are at the service of the secondary process.

Reality testing. By means of the secondary process, the ego formulates a plan for the satisfaction of the need and then tests the plan, usually by some kind of action, in order to see whether it will work. This is called reality testing.

SUPEREGO

The superego is the internalized representative of the traditional values, ideals, and moral standards of society as interpreted to the child by his parents, and enforced by means of a system of rewards and punishments imposed upon the child. The superego strives for perfection. It consists of two substructures, the **conscience** and the **ego-ideal.**

Conscience. The voice of conscience admonishes us when we violate our moral values. It makes us feel guilty.

Ego-ideal. When we behave in accordance with our ideals, we feel proud of ourselves. These feelings of pride are generated by the ego-ideal.

Instinct

An instinct is defined as an inborn psychological representation of a bodily condition. The psychological representation is called a *wish,* and the bodily excitation from which it stems is called a *need.* Thus, the state of hunger may be described in physiological terms as a condition of nutritional deficit, whereas psychologically it is represented as a wish for food. The wish acts as a motive for behavior.

Freud recognized two classes of instincts, the **life instincts** and the **death instincts.** Every instinct has a **source,** an **aim,** an **impetus,** and an **object.**

Life instincts. The life instincts serve the objectives of the survival of the individual and the propagation of the species. Hunger, thirst, and sex fall in this category.

Libido is the name Freud used to designate the form of energy which enables the life instincts to perform their work. Because Freud was primarily interested in the sex instinct, libido is often equated with sexual energy.

Death instincts. These are also called the *destructive* instincts. Freud assumed that the person has a wish to die. An important derivative of the death instincts is the *agressive* drive.

Instinct source is defined as a bodily excitation or a need.

Instinct aim is the removal of the bodily excitation.

Instinct impetus is the strength of the instinct. It is determined by the intensity of the underlying need.

Instinct object. All an individual's interactions with objects in his environment that intervene between the appearance of a wish and its fulfillment are included under the heading of instinct object. Source and aim remain constant, but the object can and does vary considerably. This means that a person can satisfy a need in many different ways.

CATHEXIS

This is a term Freud used to denote the investment of energy or libido in an object which will satisfy a need. A person is said to cathect an object that he wants.

ANTICATHEXIS

This is an inhibitory force exercised by the ego on the id. For example, a person may be strongly attracted (cathected) sexually to another person, but the ego, guided by the reality principle or by the dictates of the superego, may have to restrain the expression of the impulse.

In the final analysis, Freud believed, the dynamics of personality consist of the interplay between cathexes (driving forces) and anticathexes (restraining forces).

ANXIETY

In Freudian terms, anxiety is produced by excessive stimulation which the ego is unable to control. There are three types of anxiety: **reality anxiety, neurotic anxiety,** and **moral anxiety.**

Reality anxiety is caused by real threats and dangers from the environment.

Neurotic anxiety is the fear that the instincts in the id will break loose (overcome the anticathexes) and cause the person to do something for which he will be punished.

Moral anxiety is fear of the conscience. A person with a well-developed superego feels guilty when he does something or even things of doing something that is contrary to his moral code.

IDENTIFICATION

This concept and the following ones have to do with learning and development. We tend to identify with people, that is, to imitate some traits they have which we would like to have. A girl may choose as a model a glamorous movie star because the movie star has been successful in getting the things—fame, fortune, romance, etc.—which the girl would like to have.

DISPLACEMENT

This is probably Freud's most important developmental concept. When an instinct is blocked, that is, when it cannot secure its original object choice, the energy of the instinct is diverted (displaced) to substitute objects. For example, when a worker cannot show his anger towards his boss because he is afraid of being fired, he tends to release his anger on other persons or objects. Displacement accounts for the basic Freudian thesis that all our behavior is motivated by a few basic instincts. The sexual instinct is said by Freud to be responsible for a lot of things we do, even though many of these activities and object-choices do not appear to be sexual at all.

Freud pointed out that the development of civilization was made possible by the displacement of instinctual energy into socially acceptable and culturally creative channels. A displacement that produces a higher cultural achievement—that of an artist, for example, who paints pictures of nude females—is called a *sublimation.*

DEFENSE MECHANISMS

Under the pressure of excessive anxiety, the ego is forced to take extreme measures to relieve the pressure. These measures are called defense mechanisms, because they defend the ego against anxiety. The principal defenses are **repression, projection,** and **reaction formation.**

Repression. This is one of Freud's earliest concepts. Repression means forcing out of consciousness and into the unconscious anything that causes strong anxiety. Thus, a boy's early sexual feelings for his mother may be so threatening because he fears what his father may do to him that he represses his sexual desires. This is the place to mention Freud's concept of the **unconscious.**

Unconscious. Psychoanalysis has often been characterized as the psychology of the unconscious, and Freud has been called the first explorer of the unconscious. The unconscious comprises all the psychological material that has been repressed or that has never been permitted to become conscious. It should not be confused with Freud's concept of the **preconscious.**

Preconscious. The preconscious refers to psychological material that can become conscious when the need for it arises. It is not in a state of repression as unconscious material is. It is merely in the back of one's mind.

Projection consists of attributing to the external world something that is really in oneself. For example, it may be too painful for a person to admit that he dislikes his father. Instead, he projects his dislike into the father, and says, "My father doesn't like me."

Reaction formation refers to the replacement in consciousness of an anxiety-producing impulse or feeling by its opposite. For example, "I hate him" is replaced by "I love him."

PSYCHOSEXUAL STAGES

Freud believed that the individual passes through a series of differentiated stages in the process of becoming an adult. These stages are important for the formation of fairly permanent character traits. Freud said a person's character was pretty well established by the age of five or six. In order of appearance, the stages are the **oral,** the **anal,** the **phallic, latency,** and the **genital.**

Oral stage. During the first year of life, the baby's pleasures and frustrations revolve around the mouth. The mouth is said to be an *erogenous zone,* because pleasure is obtained from sucking, eating, and biting. Displeasure is avoided by spitting out that which is unpleasant. Adult behaviors like smoking and drinking, and adult character traits of gullibility, dependency, and sarcasm, stem from the oral period.

Anal stage. In the second year, the child is toilet-trained. This is usually his first experience with the regulation of a natural impulse and the necessity for postponing immediate gratification. The way in which toilet training is conducted by the parents and the child's reactions to it lay the foundation for a number of traits, including stubbornness, stinginess, orderliness, and destructiveness. Like the mouth, the anus is an important erogenous zone.

Phallic stage. During years three to six, sexual and aggressive feelings and fantasies associated with the genitals predominate. Two important complexes, the **Oedipus complex** and the **castration complex,** are formed in this period.

Oedipus complex. This complex, named for the Greek king who killed his father and married his mother, differs for males and females. The boy has sexual desires for the mother and aggressive feelings toward the father. The girl develops hostility toward the mother and becomes sexually attracted to the father. The girl's complex is sometimes called the *Electra complex.* The Oedipus complex lays the foundation for a person's attitudes toward persons of the same sex and of the opposite sex.

Castration complex. As a consequence of the Oedipus complex, the boy is afraid that his father will castrate him for loving the mother. The girl's castration complex takes the form of her envying the male because he has prominent genitals which she lacks. Her jealousy makes her want to deprive him of his genitals. Having a baby is supposed to be a compensation for the female's not having a penis.

Latency. This period intervenes between the end of the phallic stage and the beginning of puberty. It is a time when the sexual and aggressive impulses are relatively quiescent.

Genital stage. The oral, anal, and phallic stages are said to be *narcissistic,* because the child obtains pleasure from stimulation of his own erogenous zones: the mouth, the anus, and the genitals. During adolescence, genuine relationships with others are formed. The young person becomes transformed from a pleasure-seeking, pain-avoiding, narcissistic infant into a reality-oriented, socialized adult.

REFERENCES

Freud, S. *The Complete Psychological Works.* London: Hogarth, 23 vols., 1953–1964.

Hall, C. S. *A Primer of Freudian Psychology.* New York: New American Library, 1954.

Jones, E. *The Life and Work of Sigmund Freud.* New York: Basic Books, 3 vols., 1953–1957.

Erich Fromm

b. 1900

Freud has often been criticized for neglecting the role of society in molding man's character. Fromm has attempted to correct this oversight by showing how society shapes its members so that their needs and traits are in harmony with the aims of the society. Fromm was heavily influenced by the theories of Karl Marx, and is sometimes referred to as a Marxian personality theorist.

Erich Fromm was born in Frankfurt, Germany, on March 23, 1900. He studied psychology and sociology at the Universities of Heidelberg, Frankfurt, and Munich. After obtaining his Ph.D. in 1922 from the University of Heidelberg, he went to Berlin to receive training in psychoanalysis at the Psychoanalytic Institute there. Before coming to the United States in 1933, Fromm was associated with the influential Institute for Social Research in Frankfurt.

In the United States, he joined the International Institute for Social Research in New York City and established a private practice in psychoanalysis. Fromm now divides his time between Mexico City, where he lectures at the National University, and New York City, where he is a fellow of the William Alanson White Institute of Psychiatry, Psychoanalysis, and Psychology, and is a professor at New York University.

Fromm has written a great many books, which are widely read. His latest volume, published in 1973, is *The Anatomy of Human Destructiveness.*

One of the basic themes of Fromm's writings is that man feels lonely and alienated because he has become separated from nature and from other men. Any form of society that man has developed represents an attempt to resolve this feeling of isolation. Man lives a life of contradiction because he is both a part of nature and separate from it; he is both an animal and a human being. This dual role of being both human and animal constitutes the basic conditions of his existence. Various **needs** arise out of these conditions of existence, and these needs are realized in accordance with the social arrangements under which he lives.

The bridging concept between the individual and society is **social character.** Fromm has identified various character types that exist in Western society.

NEEDS

Man has five needs that are uniquely human. These are the need for **relatedness,** for **transcendence,** for **rootedness,** for **identity,** and for a **frame of orientation.**

Relatedness. The need for relatedness stems from the fact that man, because he can imagine and reason, has lost his instinctive relationship with nature. Consequently, man has to create his own relationships, the most satisfying one being a relationship of productive love with another human being which yields a mutuality of care, responsibility, respect, and understanding.

Transcendence. Man has a strong need to rise above his animal nature. He wants to become a creative, imaginative person rather than remaining a creature.

Rootedness is the need to feel that one is an integral part of the world, to feel that one belongs. In early childhood this need is satisfied by being close to the mother. After childhood, a person tries to satisfy this need by developing a feeling of brotherliness with other men and women.

Identity is the striving to be recognized as a unique individual, to have a sense of personal identity. Identity is achieved by one's own accomplishments or by associating oneself with another individual or with a group.

Frame of orientation is the need for a stable and consistent way of perceiving the world.

SOCIAL CHARACTER

Fromm defines social character as "the nucleus of the character structure which is shared by most members of the same culture" (1963, p. 83). The function of social character is "to shape the energies of the members of society in such a way that their behavior is not a matter of conscious decision as to whether or not to follow the social pattern, but one of *wanting to act as they have to act* and at the same time finding gratification in acting according to the requirements of the culture . . . and for the purpose of the continued functioning of the society" (1963, pp. 84–85).

Social character may express itself in a variety of forms in any given society. For example, in Western nations, these character types are found: *receptive, exploitative, hoarding, marketing,* and *productive.* The healthiest of these types is the productive.

More recently, Fromm has described another pair of character types: the *necrophilous* versus the *biophilous.* The necrophilous character is attracted to death, the biophilous character is in love with life.

REFERENCES

Fromm, E. *Escape from Freedom.* New York: Farrar and Rinehart, 1941.
Fromm, E. *Man for Himself.* New York: Rinehart, 1947.
Fromm, E. *The Chains of Illusion.* New York: Pocket Books, 1963.
Fromm, E. *Socialist Humanism.* Garden City, N.Y.: Doubleday, 1965.
Fromm, E. *The Revolution of Hope.* New York: Harper and Row, 1968.
Fromm, E. *The Anatomy of Human Destructiveness.* New York: Holt, Rinehart, and Winston, 1973.

Gestalt Psychology:

Max Wertheimer, 1880–1943
Wolfgang Köhler, 1887–1967
Kurt Koffka, 1886–1941

When psychology became established as a science in Germany in the 1870's and 1880's, it saw its main task to be the analysis of the mind into its basic elements. Gestalt psychology, which was founded shortly before the outbreak of the First World War by the German psychologists Wertheimer, Köhler, and Koffka, represented a reaction against this traditional viewpoint. Instead of looking for mental elements, they chose to study the natural configurations and patterns that appear in direct experience. Gestalt psychology also opposed Watson's behaviorism (see p. 177) for its analysis of behavior into stimulus-response elements.

The German word *"Gestalt"* refers to a specific, concrete, existing, organized entity that possesses a definite shape or form. *"Gestalten"* are the familiar objects of everyday life as they are perceived in the mind. Although Gestalt psychology initially studied perceptual wholes, especially visual figures and configurations, it subsequently extended its concepts to other psychological phenomena, such as learning, memory, thinking, and personality.

Gestalt psychology is called a *field theory,* because it considers behavior to take place in an environmental field consisting of an organized system of stresses and strains (forces) analogous to a gravitational field or an electromagnetic field.

The three founders of Gestalt psychology first came together in Frankfurt, Germany. Wertheimer was traveling by train through Germany when he got an idea for studying the problem of how we perceive motion. This problem has always been a puzzling one, because we sometimes perceive motion when there is actually no motion in the external world. Think, for example, of motion pictures and flashing signs. Wertheimer left the train at Frankfurt to buy a toy stroboscope, an instrument that causes a moving object to appear to be stationary. After making some preliminary observations in his hotel room, he went to the University of Frankfurt and asked the professor of psychology there to provide him with an experimental subject on whom he might conduct experiments. The professor suggested his assistant, Wolfgang Köhler. The following day Köhler brought his friend and fellow assistant, Kurt Koffka, and both of them took part in the experiments on the perception of motion. These experiments laid the foundation for Gestalt psychology. Wertheimer, the senior member, was then thirty years old, Köhler was twenty-three, and Koffka was twenty-four.

Max Wertheimer was born in Prague in 1880. His father was principal of a school and his mother was an accomplished musician. Wertheimer considered becoming a musician, but decided to study psychology instead. It is interesting to note that during his musical period he played chamber music with Albert Einstein. At this time Wertheimer also wrote poetry.

Wertheimer went to the University of Berlin in 1901 to study psychology, and then to the University of Wurzburg, where he obtained a Ph.D. in 1904. Because Wertheimer was financially independent, he was able to study and to do research wherever he pleased. He taught and did research at the University of Berlin from 1916 to 1929. In 1929, he became a professor at the University of Frankfurt. When Hitler rose to power, Wertheimer came to the United States, where he joined the faculty of the newly established New School for Social Research in New York City. He remained there until his death in 1943.

Wolfgang Köhler was born in Estonia on January 21, 1887, but he grew up in Germany. He took his Ph.D. at the University of Berlin in 1909, and then went to Frankfurt, where the portentous meeting with Wertheimer and Koffka took place. From 1913 to 1920 he was director of an anthropoid research station on Tenerife, the largest of the Canary Islands. There he performed his famous experiments on problem solving by chimpanzees, and developed the concept of learning by insight. In 1921 he was appointed a professor at the University of Berlin. He came to the United States in 1935, and was professor of psychology at Swarthmore College until his retirement in 1953. He died on June 11, 1967.

Kurt Koffka was born in Berlin in 1886. He received his Ph.D. from the University of Berlin in 1908, and was at the University of Frankfurt, when Wertheimer got off the train. From 1911 to 1924 he was at Giessen University. In 1924 he came to the United States, and held various positions until he was appointed professor of psychology at Smith College. He died there in 1941.

Gestalt psychology, which began as a countermovement in German psychology, became a dominant feature in the American psychological scene. Its influence is very far-reaching.

A basic concept of Gestalt psychology is the **psychophysical field,** which contains the **Ego** and the **behavioral environment.** Another basic concept is that of **figure-ground.** The figure obeys certain laws. Among the most important of these laws are those of **prägnanz** and **closure.** The figure is also subject to distortion. One distorting factor is the **figural aftereffect.** In the area of learning and problem solving, Gestalt psychology has contributed the important concept of **insight.** Gestalt psychology has made a contribution to the solution of the mind-body problem by the formulation of the concept of **isomorphism.**

PSYCHOPHYSICAL FIELD

Behavior is determined by the psychophysical field. Psychophysical means that which is both psychological and physical in nature.

Within the psychophysical field, there are the personal determinants of behavior which constitute the **Ego,** and the external determinants which constitute the **behavioral environment.**

Ego. The ego is a segregated and permanent system within the psychophysical field. The Ego has a boundary, but this boundary is not fixed. It expands to include more things (my clothes, my family, my country), and it contracts by excluding things. It is a stable organization which maintains its identity in a field of varying circumstances. It develops along the lines of becoming a better, more stable, and firmer organization or gestalt.

Behavioral environment. The behavioral environment comprises everything that is in one's conscious experience or awareness. It is determined by the distribution of forces in the geographical or physical environment. These forces or stimuli act on the sense organs, through them on the nervous system, and thence on the mind.

FIGURE-GROUND

The experienced or conscious field, that is, the behavioral environment, is differentiated into figure and ground. Think, for example, of looking at a black dot on a white piece of paper. A figure is a gestalt or organized whole which is separated from the ground by a contour or boundary. Any object or thing is a figure.

The ground serves as a framework in which the figure is suspended or on which it lies. The ground appears to be extended and continuous. It is more homogeneous, simpler, and less impressive than a figure. It is also more stable.

A figure appears to stand out from the ground. It is more substantial and compact, more strongly structured, and more impressive than the ground. A figure tries to maintain its constancy but it is altered by various factors. Among these are **prägnanz, closure,** and **figural aftereffect.**

Prägnanz. An organized whole, that is, a figure, will always be or become as regular, symmetrical, simple, and stable as prevailing conditions permit. This is the law of prägnanz.

Closure. A figure that is incomplete or open tends to be completed or closed. A circle with a gap in its circumference is seen as a completely closed circle. Closure also operates in thinking and learning. An unsolved problem or a task to be learned is an incomplete or open gestalt which creates tension in the person. By solving the problem or learning the task, closure is effected and the tension is discharged.

Figural afteraffect. If one looks fixedly at a black square for several minutes and then looks at a white square, one's perception of the white square will be distorted by the previous perception of the black square. This is an example of a figural aftereffect. It signifies that the way we perceive an object is relative to what we have just been looking at.

INSIGHT

The original meaning of this concept as described by Köhler in *The Mentality of Apes* (1956) was a sudden solution to a problem. Insight learning is contrasted with trial-and-error learning. In trial-and-error learning, the solution to a problem is learned gradually rather than suddenly. Insight is now used more broadly as a concept to describe any experience of reorganization in the total field. Reorganization means that new relationships or connections are seen.

ISOMORPHISM

This important concept has the literal meaning "similar or identical in form" without necessarily being similar in content or in the substance of which the form is made. For example, a chalk circle on the blackboard is different in substance from the pattern of light waves reflected from the chalk circle. The image formed on the retina is a different substance from the light waves, and so is the experience of a circle. But they are all alike in having the form of a circle.

Isomorphism is Gestalt psychology's answer to the mind-body problem. Form and order in experience corresponds to (is isomorphous with) form and order in the physical world, and form and order in the physiological processes. Order is not imposed by the mind on a chaotic mass of nervous impulses. The nerve impulses are not chaotic; they are organized and have form. So is the pattern of stimulation that acts on the sense organs. Order cannot arise out of disorder. Order, organization, and form prevail throughout the whole world.

REFERENCES

Koffka, K. *Principles of Gestalt Psychology.* New York: Harcourt, Brace, 1935.

Köhler, W. *Dynamics in Psychology.* New York: Liveright, 1940.

Köhler, W. *Gestalt Psychology.* New York: Liveright, rev. ed., 1947.

Köhler, W. *The Mentality of Apes.* New York: Random House, rev. ed., 1956.

Wertheimer, M. *Productive Thinking.* Enlarged edition edited by Michael Wertheimer. New York: Harper, 1959.

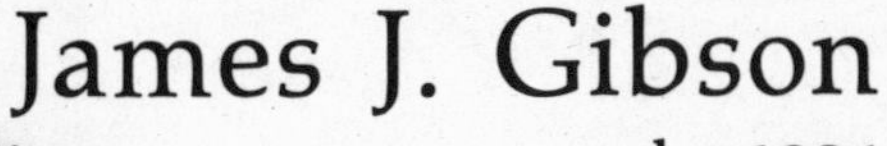

James J. Gibson

b. 1904

How do we come to know the world? This is one of the oldest questions in the history of psychology. The classical answer is as follows. The environment gives off forms of energy; for instance, light waves are reflected from objects. These forms of energy are capable of stimulating sense organs. As a consequence of sensory stimulation, nervous impulses travel to the brain, resulting in experiences that are called sensations. Sensations are welded together by association or some other intellectual process into mental representations (perceptions) of the objects of the environment. In other words, we see an object because the sensations produced by light waves coming from the object to the eyes become organized in the brain into a perception of the object.

This view of perception has been challenged by James J. Gibson of Cornell University.

James Jerome Gibson was born in McConnelsville, Ohio, on January 27, 1904. He attended Princeton University, which awarded him three degrees, a B.S. (1925), an M.A. (1926), and a Ph.D. in psychology (1928). His first academic position was at Smith College, a women's college in Northampton, Massachusetts, where he was associated with the Gestalt psychologist, Kurt Koffka (see p. 57). In 1949, Gibson became professor of psychology at Cornell University, where he is presently located. Gibson and his psychologist wife, Eleanor J. Gibson, are renowned for their experimental and theoretical work in the area of visual perception.

Gibson's answer to how we know the world is contained in his concept of **psychophysical correspondence.**

PSYCHOPHYSICAL CORRESPONDENCE

This concept states that perception is a direct function of the properties of sensory stimulation, and that stimulation (energies exciting sense organs) is a direct function of the properties of the environment and its objects. Gibson dispenses with the concept of sensation for explaining perception, and by so doing eliminates the need for an "organizer" that converts a mass of discrete sensations into a perceptual configuration of an object. Perception is not based on sensations, as older theories of perception asserted. Gibson acknowledges there are sensations, but they are so variable and changing that they could not possibly account for the fact that the environment maintains a *perceptual constancy* for us.

What accounts for perceptual constancy? Why do we recognize an object as the same object under quite different conditions of stimulation? For example, a plate is recognized as a plate even though it is sometimes seen from the side, sometimes in a tilted position, and sometimes from above. These different perspectives give off quite different patterns of stimulation. There is perceptual constancy, Gibson says, because the senses are able to detect invariant (unchanging) conditions of the light waves reflected from the object onto the eyes. Consequently, in order to understand perception, we must examine the properties of stimuli in relation to processes in the sense organs. That is what Gibson has done in his important book, *The Senses Considered as Perceptual Systems* (1966).

Gibson emphasizes the active character of perception. The sense organs do not wait to be stimulated. As perceptual systems, they search out information in the stimulus energies.

Moreover, it is Gibson's view that the different sense organs cooperate to obtain information about the world. If a sense organ is missing, as in blindness, the remaining sense organs can provide adequate information about the world.

REFERENCES

Gibson, J. J. *The Perception of the Visual World.* Boston: Houghton Mifflin, 1950.

Gibson, J. J. *The Senses Considered as Perceptual Systems.* Boston: Houghton Mifflin, 1966.

Kurt Goldstein

1878–1965

Ever since the French philosopher Descartes in the seventeenth century split the individual into two separate yet interacting entities, body and mind, attempts have been made to restore the unity of the individual. One such attempt is known as *organismic* theory. Organismic theory starts with the whole organism, and proceeds to analyze it by differentiating the whole into its constituent parts. A part is never abstracted from the whole to which it belongs and studied as an isolated entity; it is always considered as a member of the total organism. Organismic theory emphasizes the unity, integration, consistency, and coherence of the normal person. Disorganization is pathological, and is usually produced by the impact of an oppressive or threatening environment.

The leading exponent of organismic theory was Kurt Goldstein, the eminent neuropsychiatrist, whose research on brain-injured soldiers during the First World War made him famous.

Kurt Goldstein was born in Upper Silesia, Germany (now Poland), on November 6, 1878. Goldstein studied at the University of Breslau in Lower Silesia and earned a medical degree in 1903. He specialized in neurology, because his particular interest was in the field of diseases of the nervous system. He served an apprenticeship with several outstanding medical scientists for several years before accepting a teaching and research post at the Psychiatric Hospital in Königsberg, Germany. During his eight years there, Goldstein conducted extensive research and published numerous papers, which led to his appointment at the age of 36 as Professor of Neurology and Psychiatry and Director of the Neurological Institute of the University of Frankfurt. During the First World War, he became director of the Military Hospital for Brain-Injured Soldiers and was instrumental in establishing an institute for research on the aftereffects of brain injuries. It was in this institute that Goldstein made the fundamental studies which laid the foundation for his organismic viewpoint. Goldstein was also deeply influenced by Gestalt psychology (see p. 57), which was being developed in Germany at that time. In 1930, he went to the University of Berlin as a professor of neurology and psychiatry. When Hitler took over Germany, Goldstein was jailed, and then released on condition that he leave the country. He went to Amsterdam, where he wrote his most important book, *The Organism* (1939).

Coming to the United States in 1935, he worked for a year at the New York Psychiatric Institute, following which he became chief of the Laboratory of Neurophysiology at Montefiore Hospital, New York City, and a clinical professor of neurology at the College of Physicians and Surgeons of Columbia University. During this period, he lectured on psychopathology in the Department of Psychology at Columbia, and was invited to give the William James lectures at Harvard University, which were published under the title, *Human Nature in the Light of Psychopathology* (1940). During the war years, he was a clinical professor of neurology at Tufts Medical School in Boston, and published a book on the aftereffects of brain injuries. In 1945, he returned to New York City to engage in the private practice of neuropsychiatry and psychotherapy. He became associated with Columbia University and the New School for Social Research, and was guest professor at Brandeis University, where he became associated with two other organismically inclined theorists, Andras Angyal (see p. 16) and Abraham Maslow (see p. 116). Goldstein visited Germany in 1958 to examine and follow up some of the brain-injured cases he had studied during the years 1919 to 1933.

In his later years, Goldstein became more closely associated with phenomenology and existential psychology (see p. 23). He died in New York City on September 19, 1965, at the age of 86.

Goldstein's principal concept is, of course, the **organism.** The organism functions according to three dynamic concepts: **equalization, self-actualization,** and **"coming to terms" with the environment.** Goldstein also developed the important concepts of the **abstract attitude** and the **concrete attitude.**

ORGANISM

The organism is the total individual comprising both organic and psychological states and processes. It consists of differentiated members which are articulated and function as a unified whole. These parts of the organism always maintain their unity, and are inseparable except under abnormal conditions, such as strong anxiety or injury to the nervous system.

There are three kinds of behavior of the organism. These are: *performances,* which are voluntary, consciously experienced activities; *attitudes,* which are feelings, moods, and other inner experiences; and *processes,* which are bodily functions that can be experienced only indirectly.

The primary organization of organismic functioning is that of *figure* and *ground* (see p. 60). Goldstein distinguishes between *natural* figures, which are functionally embedded in a background consisting of the totality of the organism, and *unnatural* figures, which have become isolated from the total organism and whose background is also an isolated part of the organism. These unnatural figures are produced by traumatic events and by repetitive drill under conditions that are meaningless to the person. A figure is a natural one if it represents a preference on the part of the person and if the behavior which is called forth is orderly, flexible, and appropriate to the situation. It is an unnatural one if it represents a task that is imposed upon the person and if the resulting behavior is rigid and mechanical.

EQUALIZATION

Goldstein postulates an available supply of energy which is fairly constant and which tends to be evenly distributed throughout the organism. This constant, evenly distributed energy represents the "average" state of tension in the organism, and it is to this average state that the organism always returns or tries to return following a stimulus that changes the tension level. This return to an average state is the equalization process. Eating when hungry, resting when tired, and stretching when cramped are familiar examples of the equalization process. The concept of equalization explains the consistency, coherence, and orderliness of behavior in spite of disturbances. Failure to equalize may result from strong disturbances and great conflict.

SELF-ACTUALIZATION

This is Goldstein's master motive; in fact, it is the only motive the organism possesses. What appear to be different drives, such as hunger, sex, power, achievement, and curiosity, are merely different modes of actualization. Self-actualization is a universal creative impulse, although the specific aims toward which people strive vary from person to person. This is because people have different innate potentialities that shape their ends and direct the lines of their individual development, as well as different environments and cultures to which they must adjust and from which they must secure the necessary supplies for growth.

COMING TO TERMS WITH THE ENVIRONMENT

The organism and the environment have a continuous interacting relationship. The environment provides the means by which self-actualization can be achieved, but it also contains obstructions and pressures which hinder self-actualization. The environment upsets the energy balance of the organism by overstimulation, but it is also the source of energy on which the organism draws to produce equalization.

Because of the organism's dependence on the environment, the person must come to terms with the environment. Goldstein describes the normal healthy organism as one "in which the tendency towards self-actualization is acting from within, and overcomes the disturbance arising from the clash with the world, not out of anxiety, but out of the joy of conquest" (1939, p. 305). This statement suggests that coming to terms with the environment consists primarily of mastering it. If this is not possible, the person then has to adjust himself to the difficulties and realities of the external world.

ABSTRACT ATTITUDE

The normal person, Goldstein points out, is capable of differentiating between the outer world and inner experience, of planning, of seeing relationships, of reacting to organized wholes by analyzing them into their parts, of abstracting the common properties of a series of objects, and of shifting his attention from one task to another.

CONCRETE ATTITUDE

A person with a concrete attitude is incapable of doing the things, listed above, that a person with an abstract attitude can do. He cannot see relationships, he cannot abstract, he cannot plan, and so forth. He is limited to reacting to the concrete situation facing him. The concrete attitude is typical of the brain-damaged individual. Goldstein and his colleagues have devised tests for diagnosing the amount of impairment of the abstract attitude.

REFERENCES

Goldstein, K. *The Organism.* New York: American Book, 1939.

Goldstein, K. *Human Nature in the Light of Psychopathology.* Cambridge, Mass.: Harvard University Press, 1940.

Goldstein, K. *Aftereffects of Brain Injuries in War.* New York: Grune and Stratton, 1942.

Goldstein, K. *Language and Language Disturbances.* New York: Grune and Stratton, 1948.

E. R. Guthrie

1886–1959

Guthrie was an early convert to Watson's behaviorism (see p. 177) and to Pavlov's conditioned reflex (see p. 135), and remained faithful to objective psychology throughout his life.

Edwin Ray Guthrie was born in Lincoln, Nebraska, on January 1, 1886. He attended the University of Nebraska, where he obtained an A.B. in 1907 and an M.A. in 1910. He was awarded the Ph.D. by the University of Pennsylvania in 1912. Thereafter, he became an instructor in psychology at the University of Washington, where he remained until his retirement in 1956. Guthrie died in 1959.

Guthrie's theoretical viewpoint makes use of very few concepts. In fact, he recognizes only one important concept, that of **contiguity.** However, this one concept explains many psychological phenomena, especially that of learning.

CONTIGUITY

Contiguity means that two events occur close together in space and time. As applied to learning, the concept of contiguity states that an association between a stimulus and a response will be formed when they occur together or nearly together. It is not assumed that the stimulus causes the response. It is only assumed that a stimulus is present when a response is being made.

Stated in another way, a stimulus which has accompanied a response will, when the stimulus recurs, tend to be followed by the same response. The stimulus becomes a cue or signal for the response to be made. In Guthrie's words, "What is being noticed becomes the signal for what is being done" (1959). For instance, the sight of a light switch becomes the signal to press it in order to turn on the light. Unlike most other behaviorists, Guthrie does not believe that reinforcement is necessary for learning.

Guthrie points out that the stimulus which forms a connection with a response is not always the stimulus presented by the experimenter. It is often a **movement-produced stimulus.**

Movement-produced stimulus is a stimulus that results from a movement of the person's body, specifically, from movements of muscles, tendons, and joints. These movements are known technically as the kinesthetic or proprioceptive sense. For example, when an external stimulus is presented, it is often followed by a sequence of bodily movements before a final response is made. The final response then becomes associated with the last movement in the series, and not with the original stimulus that started the sequence of movements.

REFERENCES

Guthrie, E. R. *The Psychology of Learning.* New York: Harper & Row, 1935; rev. ed., 1952.

Guthrie, E. R. *The Psychology of Human Conflict.* New York: Harper & Row, 1938.

Guthrie, E. R. "Association by contiguity." In S. Koch, ed., *Psychology: A Study of a Science,* vol. II (New York: McGraw-Hill, 1959).

Donald O. Hebb

b. 1904

In 1949, the Canadian psychologist Donald Hebb published a book, *The Organization of Behavior: A Neurological Theory.* In this timely and influential volume, Hebb undertook to envisage what kinds of processes in the brain one must postulate in order to account for thinking and other psychological (mental) activities. His concepts, like those of his predecessors Pavlov (see p. 135) and Lashley (see p. 107), are neurological ones.

Donald Olding Hebb was born in Chester, Novia Scotia, on July 22, 1904. After receiving a B.A. degree from Dalhousie University in Halifax, Nova Scotia, he tried without success to write novels. Becoming interested in psychology by reading Freud, he enrolled at McGill University. There he fell under the influence of Pavlov's writings. After receiving an M.A. in 1932, he went to the University of Chicago to study with Karl Lashley, and then to

Harvard University when Lashley accepted an appointment there. Hebb received his Ph.D. in 1936 from Harvard. After holding several teaching and research positions, he became a professor of psychology at McGill University in 1948, a position he has held since that time.

Starting from the observation that thinking can be carried on for a long time with a minimum of input to the brain from the sense organs, Hebb reasoned that the brain must have its own self-governing processes that are relatively independent of stimulation from the environment. Hebb called these autonomous processes in the brain **cell assemblies.**

CELL ASSEMBLIES

A cell assembly is a system of brain cells (neurones). It is the neurological counterpart of an idea or a memory. A cell assembly consists of an intricate network of connections among the cells so that a nerve impulse can go from any cell to any other cell within the assembly. Cell assemblies may be thought of as loops or reverberating circuits. Nerve impulses traveling around these loops or circuits account for sustained thinking. The presence of alternate pathways within a cell assembly means that some of the cells can be destroyed or rendered inoperative without the functioning of the system being hindered.

A cell assembly is formed in the following manner. Any two or more cells that are repeatedly active at the same time tend to become connected, so that activity in one cell causes activity in the other cells. With continued repetition more and more cells are incorporated into the cell assembly. The formation of these connections is the neurological equivalent of learning, and the increasing number of connections is equivalent to an increase in knowledge.

A stream of thought on some subject involves a series of cell assemblies that are in **phase sequence.**

Phase sequence. Two or more cell assemblies are said to be in phase sequence when neural activity in one assembly stimulates neural activity in other assemblies. This is analogous to one idea calling forth a second idea, and the second idea calling forth a third, and so on. In other words, a stream of thought parallels activity in a sequence of cell assemblies that are in phase.

REFERENCE

Hebb, D. O. *The Organization of Behavior: A Neurological Theory.* New York: Wiley, 1949.

Fritz Heider

b. 1896

Heider is probably best-known for his concept of **structural balance,** but of equal importance are his concepts of **thing** and **medium.** These three concepts have to do with how we perceive objects and people.

Fritz Heider was born in Vienna on February 18, 1896. He received his Ph.D. in psychology from the University of Graz, in Austria. He then went to the University of Berlin, where he came under the influence of Gestalt psychology (see p. 57) and Kurt Lewin (see p. 110). In 1930, he joined the Gestalt psychologist Kurt Koffka at Smith College in Massachusetts, and stayed there until 1947, when he went to the University of Kansas, where he presently is.

THING AND MEDIUM

It is characteristic of Heider to start his theorizing from the point of view of naive psychology, that is, the way in which the ordinary person untrained in psychology experiences the world. The naive person, as well as the psychologically sophisticated person, sees *things,* not the light waves that mediate between things and the person's perception of things. Perception is an act of reconstituting a mental image of a thing from the medium of stimuli acting on sense organs. The medium provides no information in and of itself.

The perception of persons follows the same principles as the perception of things. We attribute motives, feelings, and thoughts to another person on the basis of the core perceptions we have of him. These core perceptions do not correspond to the flux of stimuli in the medium, but to the process of reconstruction that reconstitutes the stimulating medium into meaningful information. We perceive a person as trying, suffering, thinking, enjoying himself, and so forth, although there is nothing in the medium that provides this kind of information. Since the medium has nothing to do with perception, one cannot hope to arrive at an understanding of perception by analyzing the stimulating medium.

STRUCTURAL BALANCE

When you see a friend whom you regard as being an honest person acting in a dishonest manner, you are likely to feel shocked. This shock, Heider explains, is due to the state of structural imbalance between your conception of the person as being honest and your perception of his acting dishonestly.

In order to regain a state of balance, you must alter your perception. You may decide that the act is not a dishonest one, or that the person is not as honest as you thought. Another way in which balance can be achieved is to segregate the person from his act. This can be done by saying that the dishonest act was accidental, or that the person was acting under orders or under the influence of alcohol.

Here are other examples of structural imbalance. A likes B, and B likes A; balance. A dislikes B, and B dislikes A; balance. But when A likes B and B dislikes A, an unbalanced condition exists.

A more subtle illustration is the following one. A and B like each other; when they disagree about something, there is imbalance. But when A and B dislike each other, disagreement between them constitutes a balanced state, and agreement an unbalanced state.

Without much effort, the reader can think of many situations to which the concept of balance and its opposite, imbalance, apply. The concept of imbalance is similar to Festinger's concept of cognitive dissonance (see p. 40).

REFERENCES

Heider, F. *The Psychology of Interpersonal Relations.* New York: Wiley, 1958.

Heider, F. "On perception, event structure, and psychological environment." In G. S. Klein, ed., *Psychological Issues, Vol. I, Part 3* (New York: International Universities Press, 1959).

Harry Helson

b. 1898

Ever since Darwin formulated the theory of the evolution of species, psychology has been interested in studying the adaptive and maladaptive behavior of individuals. Harry Helson proposed a concept, **adaptation level,** which is a quantitative measure of the organism's adjustment to any form of stimulation.

Harry Helson was born in Chelsea, Massachusetts, on November 9, 1898. He received his bachelor's degree from Bowdoin College in 1921 and a Ph.D. in psychology from Harvard in 1924. Helson was deeply influenced by Gestalt psychology (see p. 57), and was one of its earliest expositors in the United States. He has held a number of positions in various universities, including Bryn Mawr College (1928–1949), the University of Texas (1951–1961), Kansas State University (1961–1967), and the University of Massachusetts (1968–1971). Helson is now retired and lives in Berkeley, California.

ADAPTATION LEVEL

The adaptation level (Helson also called it the *equilibrium level*) is a weighted geometric (logarithmic) average of all the stimuli acting on the organism. Helson distinguishes three classes of stimuli: **focal, background,** and **internal stimuli.**

Focal stimuli are those that are being responded to at the time.

Background stimuli are those stimulus conditions that form a context for the focal stimuli.

Internal stimuli are such things inside the individual as memories and physiological processes.

These three classes of stimuli combine to form the adaptation level. The way in which an individual responds to a new stimulus depends on his adaptation level at the time.

A simple illustration is as follows. Place one hand in cold water and the other hand in warm water. Hold them there for a few minutes. Then plunge both hands in water whose temperature is about midway between the cold and warm water. The hand that has been in warm water will feel cool; the hand that has been in cold water will feel warm. This is due to the different adaptation levels of the two hands.

In order to predict how a person is going to feel or act, one must always take into account his adaptation level at the time. If a person is feeling irritable, any slight annoyance is likely to provoke a strong reaction, but if a person is in good spirits the same annoyance will be shrugged off as being of no consequence.

REFERENCES

Helson, H. "Adaptation level theory." In S. Koch, ed., *Psychology: A Study of a Science* (New York: McGraw-Hill, 1959), I, 565–621.

Helson, H. *Adaptation-Level Theory: An Experimental and Systematic Approach to Behavior.* New York: Harper and Row, 1964.

Karen Horney

1885–1952

Karen Horney is usually referred to as a Freudian revisionist or neo-Freudian, because her concepts are elaborations and revisions of Freudian theory. Horney was one of the first promoters of a social psychology which she believed bore more relevance to personality development than Freud's concept of sexuality did.

Karen Horney was born in Hamburg, Germany, on September 16, 1885. She studied at the University of Berlin, where she received her degree in medicine. She then became associated with the Berlin Psychoanalytic Institute, and obtained her training in psychoanalysis from two of the leading figures in the field, Karl Abraham and Hanns Sachs.

In 1932, Horney accepted an invitation to come to the United States and assume the position of associate director of the Chicago Psychoanalytic Institute. She held this position for two years and then moved to New York City, where she practiced psychoanalysis and taught at the New York Psychoanalytic Institute.

Dissatisfied with the orthodox approach to psychoanalysis, Horney and others who shared the same convictions founded their own association, the Association for the Advancement of Psychoanalysis, and their own training institute, the American Institute of Psychoanalysis. Horney held the position of dean of the Institute until her death on December 4, 1952.

Horney's primary concept is that of **basic anxiety.** As a consequence of this basic anxiety, the individual develops various strategies to deal with his anxiety feelings. Some of these strategies may become such strong characteristics of the personality that they become needs. She calls these **neurotic needs** because they are not rational solutions.

BASIC ANXIETY

Basic anxiety arises from anything that interrupts or disturbs the security of the child. It is "the feeling a child has of being isolated and helpless in a potentially hostile world. A wide range of adverse factors in the environment can produce this insecurity in a child: direct or indirect domination, indifference, erratic behavior, lack of respect for the child's individual needs, lack of real guidance, disparaging attitudes, too much admiration or the absence of it, lack of reliable warmth, having to take sides in parental disagreements, too much or too little responsibility, overprotection, isolation from other children, injustice, discrimination, unkept promises, hostile atmosphere, and so on and so on" (1945, p. 41).

NEUROTIC NEEDS

Horney has described ten such needs.

Neurotic need for affection and approval. The person is compelled to please others and to live up to their expectations. His main concern is for others to have a good opinion of him. He is extremely sensitive to rejection or feelings of unfriendliness.

Neurotic need for a "partner" who will take over one's life. The person seeks a parasitic relationship with a partner who will assume responsibility for everything. He has an extreme fear of being deserted and left alone.

Neurotic need to restrict one's life within narrow borders. The person demands very little of life and prefers to live as inconspicuously as possible. He values modesty above all else, and he is always careful not to draw attention to himself.

Neurotic need for power. The desire for power is so strong that the person pursues it even if he has to harm others. Another manifestation of the craving for power is the belief in the omnipotence of will. The person feels he can achieve anything through the exercise of will power.

Neurotic need to exploit others. This need is expressed by the person's utilizing every possible advantage for personal gain by exploiting others.

Neurotic need for prestige. The person's self-evaluation is determined by the amount of public recognition he receives.

Neurotic need for personal admiration. The person has an exaggerated or inflated image of himself, and expects to be admired on the basis of this false image.

Neurotic need for personal achievement. Because of his basic insecurity, the person drives himself to greater and greater achievements.

Neurotic need for self-sufficiency and independence. Having become disappointed in his attempts to find satisfying relationships, the person refuses to become attached to anyone. He becomes a recluse or a "loner."

Neurotic need for perfection and unassailability. Because he is afraid of making mistakes for which he will be criticized, the person strives to make himself infallible. He searches for weaknesses within himself so that he can disguise or correct them before they become noticeable to others.

Horney classifies these ten neurotic needs into three groups: (1) moving *toward* people; (2) moving *away from* people; and (3) moving *against* people.

REFERENCES

Horney, K. *Neurotic Personality of Our Time.* New York: Norton, 1937.
Horney, K. *New Ways in Psychoanalysis.* New York: Norton, 1939.
Horney, K. *Our Inner Conflicts.* New York: Norton, 1945.
Horney, K. *Neurosis and Human Growth.* New York: Norton, 1950.

Clark L. Hull

1884–1952

Clark Hull was a behavioristic psychologist in the tradition of Pavlov, Watson, and Thorndike. During the 1930's and 1940's, with the assistance of several brilliant students and colleagues at the Institute of Human Relations of Yale University, Hull evolved a theory of behavior that has had great influence on several generations of psychologists.

Hull's theory is hypothetical-mathematical-deductive in form. What this means is as follows. One begins by stating assumptions about the basic laws of behavior. These assumptions are called *postulates.* From these postulates, further implications about behavior are derived. These are called *corollaries.* Then from the postulates and their corollaries precise mathematical predictions of how an individual will behave in a specific situation under specific circumstances are deduced. These predictions are called *theorems,* and may be stated as mathematical equations. If the postulates and their corollaries are true, and if the theorems have been properly derived from them, then the results of experimental tests should be in accord with the predictions.

Hull's theory of behavior focuses chiefly on such simple forms of learning as rote learning, discrimination learning, and trial-and-error learning. Like Tolman (see p. 172) and his students at Berkeley, Hull and his students at New Haven carried out their investigations mainly with laboratory rats. The use of lower animals for psychological research is based on the belief that the behavior of all mammals, rats as well as man, is governed by the same basic laws.

Clark Leonard Hull was born in a log cabin near Akron, New York, in 1884. Several years later, his family moved to a farm in Michigan, where Hull grew up and received his education. At the age of 17, he passed the teachers' examination and taught for a year in a one-room rural school. He then returned to high school and, after completing a college-preparatory course, he attended Alma College and later the University of Michigan. He decided to major in psychology after reading William James. He felt the field of psychology, since it was a young science, provided an opportunity to make original scientific discoveries. He obtained the Ph.D. from the University of Wisconsin in 1918.

After writing a pioneer work on aptitude testing and carrying out a program of research on hypnosis at the University of Wisconsin, Hull decided to devote his energies to constructing a general theory of behavior. This theory gradually took shape at the newly founded Institute of Human Relations at Yale University, where Hull went as a professor in 1929. His famous open seminar at Yale attracted a large number of students, many of whom performed the experimental work necessary to test his theoretical formulations. He and Edward Tolman were the dominant system builders in American psychology during the 1930's and 1940's. Although both theories were behavioristic, the concepts developed by Hull differed markedly from those set forth by Tolman.

Hull described his theory in three books, *Principles of Behavior* (1943), *Essentials of Behavior* (1951), and *A Behavior System* (1952).

Hull died on May 10, 1952, shortly after completing the manuscript of his third book.

Hull's student and closest associate at Yale was Kenneth Spence (1907–1967). Spence was intimately involved with Hull in the formulation of Hull's viewpoint, so much so that it is sometimes referred to as the Hull-Spence theory. During his long tenure as a professor at the State University of Iowa, 1938–1965, Spence was the leading proponent and developer of neo-behaviorism. Through his research, his writings, and the many students who were influenced by him, Spence became a dominant figure in American psychology.

Hull's scientific credo is summed up in the following quotation. "I came to the definite conclusion around 1930 that psychology is a true natural science; that its primary laws are expressible quantitatively by means of a moderate number of ordinary equations; that all the complex behavior of single individuals will ultimately be derivable as secondary laws from (1) these primary laws together with (2) the conditions under which behavior occurs; and that all the behavior of groups as a whole, that is, strictly social behavior as such, may similarly be derived as quantitative laws from the same primary equations." (1952b, p. 155).

Hull's theory of behavior identifies the variables that intervene between stimulus and response. The most important intervening variable in his system is **reaction potential.** The strength of the potential for making a given response to a given stimulus is determined by five factors: **drive, stimulus intensity, incentive motivation, habit strength,** and **inhibitory potential.** Several of these concepts have subconcepts under them. Other important concepts of what intervenes between stimulus and response are **stimulus generalization, inhibitory generalization, goal gradient, fractional antedating goal reaction, habit family hierarchy,** and **stimulus trace.**

REACTION POTENTIAL

Reaction potential is the potential that an organism possesses at a given moment for making a particular response when a stimulus is presented. The strength of this potential determines the probability of making the response. When the potential is weak, the probability is low that the response will be made; when the potential is strong, the probability is high that the response will be made.

The strength of the reaction potential is the product of four variables: **drive, stimulus intensity, incentive motivation,** and **habit strength.** From the product of these four components, there is subtracted the amount of **inhibitory potential** present in the organism at the time.

Drive is any primary motive or need, such as hunger, or any **secondary motivation.**

Secondary motivation. When a neutral stimulus is associated with a primary drive, the neutral stimulus acquires the characteristic of a drive. This is known as secondary motivation.

Stimulus intensity is the strength of the stimulus. An organism is more likely to respond to a stimulus of high intensity, for example, a loud noise, than to one of low intensity.

Incentive motivation refers to the amount of reward that is given the individual, for example, the amount of food given to a hungry organism.

Habit strength depends on the number of times a particular stimulus-response connection has received either **primary** or **secondary reinforcement.**

Primary reinforcement is anything that reduces the strength of a drive, for example, eating food by a hungry person.

Secondary reinforcement is a neutral stimulus that has acquired, from association with a drive-reduction situation, the capability of serving as a reinforcing agent. For example, objects that are present when a hungry organism is eating tend to become secondary reinforcers.

Inhibitory potential. When an individual makes a certain response, there is a resistance to repeating the same response again for a time. Each time he repeats the response, the resistance builds up. This is known as inhibitory potential. The amount of inhibitory potential is subtracted from the amount of reaction potential in order to determine the effective reaction potential.

STIMULUS GENERALIZATION

The habit strength attached to a stimulus-response unit tends to generalize to other, similar stimuli. This means a person will react to a new stimulus in the same way that he has learned to react to a previous stimulus if the two stimuli resemble each other. Thus, if a person has developed a fear of snakes, this fear tends to generalize to other snakelike animals or objects.

INHIBITORY GENERALIZATION

The tendency not to react to a stimulus can also generalize to other, similar stimuli. This is known as inhibitory generalization. If a child has learned not to contradict his parents, he will tend not to contradict other persons with authority, for example, teachers.

GOAL GRADIENT

The longer the time interval is between making a response and receiving a reinforcement, the less effect the reinforcement has on the habit strength. This explains why, in a series of responses which lead to a rewarding goal, the responses near the goal are learned first, and those near the beginning are learned last.

FRACTIONAL ANTEDATING GOAL REACTION

This is also called a *fractional anticipatory goal reaction.* If a person is learning a sequence of stimulus-response units in order to reach a desired goal, the final, rewarded response tends to generalize to earlier stimuli in the sequence. This means that he will make the same response to earlier stimuli that he does to the final goal stimulus. In other words, the learner anticipates that he will reach the goal earlier if he makes the goal response to stimuli early in the sequence.

HABIT-FAMILY HIERARCHY

When there are several ways to reach a goal, and when these alternatives vary in distance and work required, a person learns eventually to take the shortest and least laborious path.

STIMULUS TRACE

The effects of a stimulus do not cease immediately after the stimulus is removed. These effects persist in the form of a trace; presumably this trace is located in the nervous system. This explains why a stimulus-response connection can be strengthened by a reinforcement that is given after the stimulus is no longer acting on the person.

REFERENCES

Hull, C. L. *Principles of Behavior.* New York: Appleton-Century-Crofts, 1943.

Hull, C. L. *Essentials of Behavior.* New Haven: Yale University Press, 1951.

Hull, C. L. *A Behavior System: An Introduction to Behavior Theory Concerning the Individual Organism.* New Haven: Yale University Press, 1952a.

Hull, C. L. "Autobiography." In *A History of Psychology in Autobiography* (Worcester, Mass.: Clark University Press, 1952b), vol. IV.

Kendler, H. H., and J. T. Spence, eds. *Essays in Neobehaviorism: A Memorial Volume to Kenneth W. Spence.* New York: Appleton-Century-Crofts, 1971.

Spence, K. W. *Behavior Theory and Conditioning.* New Haven, Conn.: Yale University Press, 1956.

Spence, K. W. *Behavior Theory and Learning.* Englewood Cliffs, N.J.: Prentice-Hall, 1960.

William James
1842–1910

William James is generally considered to be America's greatest psychologist. This distinction is based almost solely on his two-volume work *Principles of Psychology*, which was published in 1890. For years, these two volumes and a briefer one-volume edition were the leading psychology textbooks. Not only did the *Principles* survey all that was known about scientific psychology at the time, but, more importantly, every sentence in it bears the imprint of James' vivid personality and lively mind. It is an exciting and beautifully written book, which has been an inspiration for generations of students and psychologists.

William James was born into an intellectual family in New York City on January 11, 1842. His father was a writer on religious topics and a close friend of Ralph Waldo Emerson and other prominent nineteenth century figures. James' brother, Henry, became a celebrated novelist. When James was eighteen, he decided to become a painter, but he soon learned that he did not have the necessary talent. He entered Harvard in 1861 and received a medical degree in 1869. He never practiced medicine, however. As a young man James was plagued by illness and depression, and traveled in Europe seeking a cure for his condition. During this period, he made friends with many of the leading scientists and philosophers in Europe. When James returned to the United States, he was invited to teach physiology at Harvard, but he turned more and more to psychology. James established a small psychological laboratory at Harvard and had a profound influence on many students who became psychologists. In his later years, James devoted most of his attention to philosophy. His major contributions to philosophy consisted of the viewpoints known as pragmatism and radical empiricism. He was also interested in the psychology of religion, and wrote a classic in this field, *Varieties of Religious Experience* (1902). He was also deeply involved with psychical research, known now as parapsychology. James died on August 26, 1910.

James did not formulate a psychological system; yet a number of his ideas helped to form the mainstream of modern psychlogical thought and are still viable today. The concepts we shall discuss are **habit, stream of consciousness, self, emotion,** and **will.**

HABIT

The chapter on habit in the *Principles* is a very famous one. James called habit "the enormous fly-wheel of society. . . . it keeps the fisherman and the deck-hand at sea through the winter; it holds the miner in his darkness, and nails the countryman to his log-cabin and his lonely farm through all the months of snow. . . ." (1962, pp. 158–159). Habit is the mechanism of conformity, custom, and conservatism.

Habit, James said, is a fixed pathway in the brain connecting a sense organ which has been stimulated with a set of muscles whose movements constitute an act. These pathways are deepened by use. The chief advantage of habit is that it diminishes the need for conscious control, since a habitual act becomes an automatic one.

STREAM OF CONSCIOUSNESS

Consciousness, James asserted, does not consist of discrete, distinctive, and disconnected mental elements; it is flowing continuously like a stream. Even when the stream halts temporarily because the person is asleep or unconscious, what follows the gap seems to belong to and be continuous with what preceded the gap. The stream of consciousness provides a medium in which every thought, image, and feeling is immersed. This means that a thought flows out of a past and toward a future. It also means that every thought is affected by the nature of the medium in which it is immersed.

This concept was responsible for the appearance of a new literary movement known as "stream of consciousness" writing, exemplified by Gertrude Stein, who had studied with James.

SELF

James' chapter on the self set the stage for contemporary discussions of this concept. James distinguished between the self-as-known—*the empirical Me*—and the self-as-knower—the *Ego* or I. The empirical Me contains everything that a person can call his. There are three aspects of the empirical Me: the *material,* consisting of my body, my clothes, my home, my family, and my possessions; the *social,* which is the recognition I get from others; and the *spiritual,* comprising my states of consciousness, my traits, my attitudes, and my dispositions. There are as many social Me's as there are people who recognize me.

With regard to the self-as-knower, the I, James felt there is no need to assume a soul or a spirit or a little person inside the head that is the I who thinks, feels, and acts. For James, this I is nothing more or less than the stream of consciousness. Thoughts are not thought by an I; they are the I.

EMOTION

James' concept of emotion is discussed in almost every introductory psychology textbook. Because this concept was formulated independently by a Danish physiologist, Carl Lange, it is customarily referred to as the James-Lange theory of emotions.

James proposed that when we experience an emotion, the experience is caused not by our perception of the situation, but by the bodily changes which result from stimulation. Suppose a person receives word he has been awarded a valuable prize. The news itself is not sufficient to make him feel joyful. It has to stir his body before he experiences the emotion of joy. In James' words, we do not laugh because we are happy and weep because we are sad. We are happy because we laugh, and we are sad because we weep.

WILL

Does man have free will? James said this is not a question for psychology but for philosophy. However, will or volition is a very important psychological concept. The essential feature of will is a concentrated effort of attention. What we concentrate on is not the act we wish to perform, but the idea or image of an act and its consequences. Once the idea is fully developed, the act will follow as a matter of course. This is known as *ideo-motor action.*

Many voluntary acts are carried out almost without thinking because they have become habitual. Other voluntary acts require deliberation among alternatives before a final decision is made. In order to act wisely, one must have a large stock of ideas of the various acts that are possible and knowledge of the consequences of each of the acts. This stock of ideas is acquired through experience.

REFERENCES

James, W. *Principles of Psychology.* Two volumes. New York: Holt, 1890.

James, W. *Psychology: Briefer Course.* New York: Holt, 1892; Crowell-Collier, paperback, 1962.

James, W. *Varieties of Religious Experience.* New York: Longmans, Green, 1902. New Hyde Park, N.Y.: University Books, 1963.

Perry, R. B. *The Thought and Character of William James.* Two volumes. Boston: Little, Brown, 1935.

C. G. Jung
1875–1961

Jung became associated with Freud (see p. 42) during the early years of the psychoanalytic movement, and was the first president of the International Psychoanalytic Association. In 1914, he resigned from the Association in order to develop his own viewpoint, which became known as *analytical psychology.*

Carl Gustav Jung was born in the village of Kesswil on Lake Constance in Switzerland on July 26, 1875. His father was a Swiss Reform pastor, as were eight of his uncles. During his childhood, Jung played by himself, since his sister was nine years younger. His mother suffered from a nervous disorder which made her inaccessible much of the time, and his father was irritable and difficult to get along with. Jung's teen-age years were characterized by confusion and inquisitiveness, especially about religion. However, his religious conflicts were eventually displaced by other intellectual interests.

When Jung enrolled at Basel University, he had not decided what to major in, but partly as a result of several occult experiences he had at the time, he decided to become a psychiatrist. After receiving his medical degree in 1900, Jung became an assistant at the Burghölzli Mental Hospital in Zurich, where he was associated with the renowned psychiatrist Eugen Bleuler. In 1902, Jung spent several months studying with the prominent French psychiatrist Pierre Janet. The greatest influence on Jung's thinking, however, was Sigmund Freud. Jung read Freud's *The Interpretation of Dreams* soon after it was published in 1900, and after a period of correspondence, Jung went to Vienna to meet and talk with Freud. This was the beginning of a close personal and professional relationship that lasted for six years. Their friendship was finally terminated for several reasons, a chief one being that Jung refused to place as much emphasis on sex as Freud did.

In 1905 Jung became lecturer in psychiatry at the University of Zurich and senior physician at the Psychiatric Clinic. At the same time he conducted a private practice, which eventually required so much time that he had to resign his Clinic appointment. While Jung was at the Clinic, he established a laboratory for studying mental patients using the word-association test. These studies gained for him a worldwide reputation, and in 1909 he was invited to give lectures on his findings at Clark University in Worcester, Massachusetts. Freud was also invited to lecture, and the two of them traveled to the United States together. This was the first of many visits Jung made to the United States. He also traveled extensively and made studies of the psychology of primitive people.

Jung was a devoted student of the psyche. He spent his entire adult lifetime right down to the day of his death studying, investigating, and writing. His collected works fill nineteen volumes. He wrote not only on psychology and psychotherapy, but also on religion, mythology, social problems, art and literature, and such occult subjects as alchemy, astrology, telepathy and clairvoyance, yoga, spiritualism, fortune telling, and flying saucers. He was particularly interested in the symbolism of alchemy. Jung and Freud are often considered to be the two most important figures in modern psychology.

Jungian analytical institutes for the training of analysts are located in cities throughout the world. The mecca of analytical psychology remains in Zurich, where the C. J. Jung Institute was founded in 1948.

Everyone who came into personal contact with Jung was struck by his joviality, the twinkle in his eyes, his hearty, infectious laugh, and his wonderful sense of humor. Physically he was tall, broad-shouldered, and strong. He was a mountain climber and expert sailor. His home was located on the shores of Lake Zurich. He enjoyed gardening, splitting wood, chiseling stone, building, and other manual activities. He liked to play games. He was a devoted husband and the father of five children. Jung was an active, vigorous, healthy man.

Jung died on June 6, 1961, at the age of 85. In the year of his death there was published an autobiography, *Memories, Dreams, Reflections* (1961). It is primarily an inner or spiritual autobiography. The tone of the book is set by the first sentence, "My life is a story of the self-realization of the unconscious."

In Jungian psychology the whole personality is referred to as the **psyche.** The psyche is made up of three components: the conscious **ego,** the **personal unconscious** and its **complexes,** and the **collective unconscious** and its **archetypes.**

Important dynamic concepts are **psychic energy** or **libido, value, entropy,** and **equivalence.** Developmental concepts are those of **individuation,** the **transcendent function,** and **symbolization.** Jung also devised a typology that has been very influential. It consists of the **attitudes** of **extraversion** and **introversion,** and the psychological **functions** of **thinking, feeling, sensing,** and **intuiting.** Finally, there is his concept of **synchronicity.**

PSYCHE

The psyche embraces all thoughts, feelings, and other psychological states and processes, both conscious and unconscious.

Ego. The ego is the conscious mind.

Personal unconscious is a region adjoining the ego. It contains experiences that were once conscious but that have been repressed, suppressed, forgotten, or ignored, and experiences that were too weak in the first place to make a conscious impression on the person.

Complex. A complex is an organized group or constellation of feelings, thoughts, perceptions, and memories which exists in the personal unconscious. A complex is usually organized around some significant person, as in the mother or father complex, or some significant object, as in a money complex. The nucleus of the complex acts as a kind of magnet, attracting to it various related experiences. A complex can become very powerful and even act as a separate personality.

Collective unconscious. Unlike the personal unconscious, the collective unconscious does not acquire its contents from personal experience. The contents of the collective unconscious are inherited, and they are the same for everyone. The collective unconscious is the psychic residue of man's evolutionary development, a residue that accumulates as a consequence of repeated experiences over many generations. The components of the collective unconscious are called **archetypes.**

Archetype. An archetype is a universal idea or image which contains a large element of emotion. It is a permanent deposit in the mind of an experience that has been constantly repeated for many generations. For example, ever since man has been man, he has seen the sun make its daily excursion from one horizon to the other. The repetition of this impressive experience eventually became fixed in the collective unconscious as an archetype of the sun-god or a supreme deity.

Although all archetypes, and there are many of them, may be thought of as systems that are relatively independent of the rest of the psyche, some archetypes have evolved so far as to warrant their being treated as separate systems within the psyche. These are the **persona,** the **anima** and **animus,** the **shadow,** and the **self.**

Persona. The persona is a mask which is adopted by an individual in response to the demands of social convention. The purpose of the mask is to make an impression upon others and often to conceal one's true feelings and thoughts.

Anima and animus. The anima refers to the feminine side of a man's nature, and the animus refers to the masculine side of a woman's nature.

Shadow. The shadow archetype consists of the animal

instincts which man inherited in his evolution from lower forms of life. The shadow typifies the animal side of the psyche.

Self. The self represents the individual's striving for unity, wholeness, and completeness. It is the center of the psyche, around which all the other systems revolve. The development of the self is life's goal, a goal that people constantly strive for but rarely attain. Before the self can emerge, the various components of the psyche must become fully developed.

PSYCHIC ENERGY (LIBIDO)

The work of the psyche is performed by means of psychic energy or libido. Psychic energy originates in the same way that all vital energy does, namely, from the metabolic processes of the body.

VALUE

The amount of psychic energy invested in an element of the personality is called the value of that element. Value is a measure of intensity. When we speak of placing a high value on a particular idea or feeling or act, we mean that we will expend a lot of energy in developing the idea or expressing the feeling or performing the act.

EQUIVALENCE

The equivalence principle states that if a particular value weakens or disappears, the sum of energy represented by the value will not be lost from the psyche, but will reappear in a new value. A person who loses an interest in some activity will find that a new interest has taken its place.

ENTROPY

The entropy principle states that the distribution of energy throughout the psyche seeks an equilibrium or balance. If two values are of unequal intensity, energy will tend to pass from the stronger value into the weaker value until a balance is reached. Or if the persona is overdeveloped and the shadow is underdeveloped, energy will tend to pass from the persona into the shadow.

INDIVIDUATION

This is Jung's most important developmental concept. As noted before, the psyche has a tendency to develop in the direction of a stable unity. In order to realize this aim, the various components that make up the psyche must become completely differentiated and fully developed. This process of differentiation and development Jung calls individuation.

TRANSCENDENT FUNCTION

When development and differentiation have been achieved by the operation of the individuation process, the individuated systems are then integrated by the transcendent function. This function is endowed with the capacity to unite all the opposing trends within the psyche and to strive toward the ideal goal of perfect wholeness, or what Jung calls *selfhood.* This desire for wholeness is found in dreams, myths, and other symbolic representations.

SYMBOLIZATION

Man lives in a world of symbols which become richer and more complex as the individual grows older. A symbol in Jungian psychology has two major functions. On the one hand, it represents an attempt to satisfy an instinctual impulse which has been frustrated; on the other hand, it is an embodiment of an archetype.

Symbols are representations of the psyche. They not only express the stored-up racial and individually acquired wisdom of mankind, but can also represent levels of development that are far ahead of man's present status. Man needs symbols in order to develop.

ATTITUDE

An attitude is the way in which the individual orients himself toward the inner and outer worlds. There are two major attitudes, **extraversion** and **introversion.**

Extraversion. The extraverted attitude orients the person toward the external, objective world. A person who invests a lot of libido in things outside himself is called an *extravert.*

Introversion. In introversion, libido flows towards subjective psychic processes. A person who lives within himself is called an *introvert.*

FUNCTIONS

There are four fundamental psychological functions: **thinking, feeling, sensation,** and **intuition.**

Thinking. By thinking man tries to understand the world and himself. It consists of connecting ideas with each other in order to arrive at a general concept or a solution to a problem. Thinking is called a rational function.

Feeling is an evaluative function; it either accepts or rejects an idea, on the basis of whether the idea arouses a pleasant or an unpleasant feeling. Feeling, like thinking, is also a rational function, because it makes use of judgment.

Sensation is sense perception, which comprises all conscious experiences produced by stimulation of the sense organs. It yields concrete facts. Sensation is called an irrational function, because it does not require reasoning.

Intuition is like sensation, in being an experience which is immediately given rather than produced by thought or feeling. Intuition differs from sensation because the person who has an intuition does not know where it came from or how it originated. It appears "out of the blue." Intuition is also an irrational function.

A person does not use all four of these functions in equal proportions. He tends to use one more than the others. This is called the *superior function.* The one he uses least is called the *inferior function.*

The attitudes and functions combine in various ways to create *psychological types.* One person may be a predominantly extraverted feeling type; another person may be an introverted intuitive type. Ideally, the attitudes and functions should all be fully individuated in order to produce a well-balanced person.

SYNCHRONICITY

The principle of causality states that every event has a cause. Jung formulated another scientific principle, which he called synchronicity. Two events that are related in meaning may occur at the same time without one being the cause of the other. For example, I may be thinking of a friend I have not seen or heard from for a long time when the postman arrives with a letter from him. A person may dream of the death of a relative, and learn later that the relative died at the same time he had the dream. Mental telepathy, clairvoyance, and other forms of paranormal experiences are to be explained by the principle of synchronicity, according to Jung.

REFERENCES

Hall, C. S., and V. J. Nordby. *A Primer of Jungian Psychology.* New York: Taplinger, 1973; New American Library, paperback, 1973.

Jung, C. G. *Collected Works.* Edited by H. Read, M. Fordham, and G. Adler. Princeton, N.J.: Princeton University Press, 1953–.

Jung, C. G. *Memories, Dreams, Reflections.* New York: Random House, 1961.

George A. Kelly

1905–1966

George Kelly was head of the clinical psychology program at Ohio State University and a practicing clinical psychologist for many years. During that time he formulated a theory of personality, based on his observations of persons undergoing psychotherapy, which he called a psychology of personal constructs.

Kelly also developed a technique of psychotherapy that went hand in hand with his theory. This is called *fixed-role therapy.* The therapist assigns a role to the client which the client acts out over a period of time. The role assigned is based on diagnostic interviews and tests, and is one that is supposed to resolve the problems of the client by substituting a new, effective personality for an old, ineffective one.

Kelly also devised a test for getting at the personal constructs of an individual. This is called the *Repertory or Rep test.*

George Alexander Kelly was born in Perth, Kansas, on April 28, 1905. His undergraduate education was obtained at Friends College and Park College, with majors in physics and mathematics. For a brief period, he was an aeronautical engineer. After being awarded a master's degree in educational sociology from the University of Kansas in 1928, he taught in a labor college and conducted speech and Americanization classes. He then decided to study psychology at the State University of Iowa, which awarded him the Ph.D. in 1931. During this time he was also an exchange student at the University of Edinburgh and earned a bachelor of education.

For ten years after receiving his doctorate, Kelly was on the faculty of Fort Hayes Kansas State College. During the war he was an aviation psychologist. After the war he joined the faculty of the University of Maryland for a year, and then went to Ohio State University to replace Carl Rogers (see p. 147) as head of the clinical psychology program. During this time he wrote his important book, *The Psychology of Personal Constructs* (1955). In 1965 Kelly went to Brandeis University, where he died in March, 1966.

The central concept in Kelly's theory is that of **personal constructs.**

PERSONAL CONSTRUCTS

A personal construct is the way in which an individual construes, interprets, or attaches meaning to some aspect of the world, including himself. For example, a person may possess the construct that college students are radicals or that snakes are dangerous or that he is a failure. A construct is like a belief or an attitude. It is not always possible, however, for a person to put a construct into words.

The importance of a personal construct is that it determines what and how a person will perceive, remember, learn, think, and act with respect to the class of elements that are encompassed by the construct. If he has the construct that all snakes are dangerous, he will try to avoid them. A construct may be thought of as a working hypothesis which is validated or invalidated by the test of experience. One tends to revise constructs in the general direction of greater validity, although sometimes a person stubbornly clings to a construct in the face of evidence to the contrary.

A construct is a way of thinking which construes some elements as being alike and yet different from other elements. For example, a person may feel that a particular breed of dogs is vicious, whereas another breed is docile. A construct is a way of seeing likenesses and differences. The development of a construct requires abstracting common elements from among a group of objects or persons, discriminating them from other elements, and forming a generalization about the common elements. This generalization is the construct.

Constructs are always dichotomous; that is, they include certain elements while excluding all other elements. An animal is either a dog or it is not a dog. A person is either my friend or not my friend. When a person performs an act or a series of acts, each act represents a choice between dichotomous constructs.

Constructs enable us to anticipate the future by virtue of the fact that events to which a construct applies recur over and over again. This means that our constructs tend to remain fairly constant. They do undergo change, however, and new constructs are added as a consequence of new experiences. New experiences can cause one to look at the world in a fresh way. It is one of the aims of psychotherapy—its chief aim, Kelly would say—to change the constructs of a person, either because they are invalid or because they are too narrow or too broad in scope.

The totality of a person's constructs constitutes what Kelly calls his *construction system.*

Constructs can be classified in various ways: as **impermeable, permeable, preemptive, constellatory, propositional, broad, constricted, core, peripheral, tight,** and **loose.**

Impermeable constructs are those that apply to a specific set of elements to which no new elements are admitted. It is a closed system.

Permeable constructs are open to the addition of new elements.

Preemptive constructs do not permit their elements to belong to any other construct. For example, anything that is a ball can be nothing other than a ball.

Constellatory constructs confer fixed and unalterable characteristics on their elements. For example, if this object is a ball, it must be round, resilient, and small enough to hold in the hand. If it does not have these characteristics or if it has other ones, it does not belong to the construct ball.

Propositional constructs permit their elements to belong to other constructs as well. A ball may be an element in another construct as well as being an element in the construct ball.

Broad constructs include many elements. For example, modern art is ugly.

Constricted constructs include few elements, sometimes only one element. For example, John is my only friend.

Core constructs are those that refer to oneself. They maintain one's identity and the continuity of one's existence. Once formed they are difficult to change. Inappropriate core constructs pose many difficulties for the individual.

Peripheral constructs are those that can be altered fairly easily without disturbing the core constructs.

Tight constructs lead to fixed, unvarying predictions or anticipations. For example, if a person has the construct that people with red hair have quick tempers, he will always act in the same way toward red-haired persons. He will expect them to lose their tempers easily.

Loose constructs permit predictions to vary, depending on the situation and other factors.

REFERENCE

Kelly, G. A. *The Psychology of Personal Constructs.* Two volumes. New York: Norton, 1955.

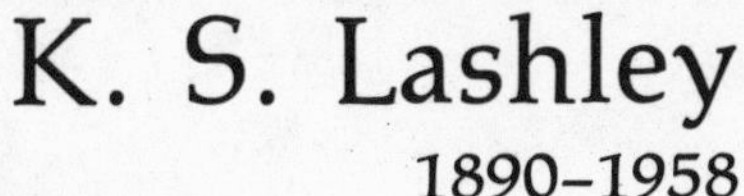

K. S. Lashley

1890–1958

For many years, scientists regarded the brain as a switchboard whose function is to make connections between the receiving organs, the senses, and the acting organs, the muscles. The brain, it was thought, contributed little to the determination of behavior. The work of Karl Lashley in the 1920's established a new conception of the brain.

Karl Spencer Lashley was born in Davis, West Virginia, in 1890. His father was a store owner and banker. His mother was an avid reader and possessed a library of 2,000 volumes. Lashley became interested in zoology at the University of West Virginia, from which he graduated in 1910. He then went to the University of Pittsburgh as a teaching fellow in zoology, receiving his M.A. in 1911. While at Pittsburgh, he took the only course in psychology he ever had. He continued his studies in zoology at Johns

Hopkins University and was awarded the doctorate in 1914. At Johns Hopkins, he became acquainted with John Watson (see p. 177) and was greatly influenced by Watson's behaviorism. He also observed brain-injured patients with S. I. Franz, and it was this experience that set the course of his later experimental work. Lashley held teaching and research positions at the University of Minnesota (1917–1926), the University of Chicago (1929–1935), and Harvard University from 1935 until his death in 1958.

Lashley was not interested in formal teaching and did very little of it. He believed if a student wanted to learn a subject, he would learn it through his own efforts with minimal guidance from an instructor. He was always helpful, however, to students engaged in their own research and studies. Lashley did his own research himself—constructing apparatus, performing operations, running rats in mazes, and analyzing the results—instead of having it done by assistants, as is so often the case today. One of his most brilliant students was D. O. Hebb (see p. 73).

As a result of a long series of experiments in which rats with injuries (lesions) in various regions of the cerebral cortex learned mazes and other tasks, Lashley proposed two concepts which revolutionized thinking about the way in which the brain functions. These concepts are **equipotentiality** and **mass action.**

EQUIPOTENTIALITY

Lashley used the term "equipotentiality" in the sense of equal capacity for performing a psychological activity, such as learning to make a discrimination between two visual stimuli. He said that the cerebral cortex or regions therein are equipotential, by which he meant that if a part of the cortex is destroyed, another part could assume the function of the destroyed part.

For example, rats were trained to make a visual discrimination. Lesions were then made in the region of the cortex that serves vision. After the lesions were made, the rats could no longer make the discrimination that they had previously learned. They could, however, relearn the discrimination by utilizing a different part of the brain. The undamaged part of the visual cortex is said to be equipotential with that which had been destroyed. Many such experiments were performed by Lashley.

MASS ACTION

This concept is closely related to equipotentiality. Simply stated, the concept of mass action says that in any fairly complex learning situation, the whole cortex, or large areas of the cortex, is involved. This concept is exemplified in the following type of experiment. Rats with varying amounts of cortical destruction learned a maze. Those rats which had little of the cortex destroyed learned it as readily as rats without any cortical lesions. The larger the amount of damage to the cortex, the slower the learning.

The concepts of equipotentiality and mass action refuted the idea that learning and other psychological processes are dependent on fairly localized structural regions in the cortex. For complex learning and thinking, it may be said that the whole cortex is utilized.

REFERENCE

Lashley, K. S. *Brain Mechanisms and Intelligence.* Chicago: University of Chicago Press, 1929. New York: Hafner, reprinted ed., 1963.

Kurt Lewin
1890–1947

Kurt Lewin is known for the formulation of a field theory of psychology. Lewin's field theory holds that the behavior of a person is a function of a field of interrelated conditions and forces that exist at the time the behavior occurs. This theory has stimulated a great amount of research, and has had wide application in the areas of personality, social psychology, child psychology, and industrial psychology.

Kurt Lewin was born on September 9, 1890, in a small village in the Prussian province of Posen. He was the second of four children. His father owned and operated a general store. The family moved to Berlin in 1905, where Lewin completed his schooling. He entered the University of Freiburg, planning to study medicine, but he soon gave up this idea and, after a semester at the University of Munich, returned to Berlin in 1910 and matriculated at the University there to study for a doctorate in psychology. His major professor was Carl Stumpf, a highly respected experimental psychologist. Upon completing requirements for the doctorate in 1914, Lewin served in the German army for four years as an infantryman, rising from private to lieutenant. At the end of the war, he returned to the University of Berlin as an instructor and a research assistant in the Psychological Institute. He was a stimulating teacher, and students flocked to his classes and engaged in research under his supervision.

At the University of Berlin he was associated with two of the founders of Gestalt psychology, Max Wertheimer and Wolfgang Köhler (see p. 57). He was influenced by their viewpoint, but did not become a Gestalt psychologist. He was also influenced by Freudian psychoanalysis (see p. 42). In 1926, he was promoted to a professorship. While at the University of Berlin, Lewin and his students published a series of brilliant experimental and theoretical papers.

When Hitler came to power, Lewin was a visiting professor at Stanford University. He returned briefly to Germany to settle his affairs, and then returned to the United States, where he resided the rest of his life. He was professor of child psychology at Cornell University for two years (1933–1935), before being called to the State University of Iowa as professor of psychology in the Child Welfare Station. In 1954, Lewin accepted an appointment as professor and director of the Research Center for Group Dynamics at the Massachusetts Institute of Technology. At the same time, he became director of the Commission of Community Interrelations of the American Jewish Congress, which engaged in research on community problems. He died suddenly of a heart attack in Newtonville, Massachusetts, February 12, 1947, at the age of 56.

During his years in the United States, he attracted a large number of graduate students, many of whom have become prominent psychologists. As a person, Lewin was very democratic, friendly, energetic, and immensely stimulating. He made a lasting impression on everyone who came into contact with him. His influence on psychology, it is commonly agreed, was a very great one.

Lewin's most important concept is that of the **life space,** which includes a **person** surrounded by a **psychological environ-**

ment. The person and the psychological environment are divided into **regions** which undergo **differentiation** with age. Regions of the environment are said to be connected when a person can perform a **locomotion** between the regions. Regions of a person are said to be connected when a **communication** can take place between them. These concepts are often referred to inclusively as *topological psychology.*

The region which lies just outside the life space is the **foreign hull.** The study of the foreign hull is known as *psychological ecology.*

Lewin's most important motivational concept is that of **need.** Needs are responsible for creating **tension systems** within the person, for imparting positive and negative **valences** to the psychological environment, and for applying pressures or **vectors** on the individual. These concepts are referred to collectively as *vector psychology.*

Three additional concepts of importance are those of **level of aspiration, conflict,** and **group dynamics.**

LIFE SPACE

This is Lewin's most general concept and the starting point of his theory. The life space embraces the totality of possible psychological facts or circumstances that are capable of determining the behavior of an individual in a concrete situation. The life space consists of two **regions,** the **person** and the **psychological environment.** Surrounding the life space but separated from it by a boundary is the **foreign hull.** The foreign hull comprises all those nonpsychological factors that may penetrate and affect the life space.

Person. The person is a differentiated region in the life space and is set apart from the psychological environment by a boundary. The structure of the person consists of an outer region called the *perceptual-motor region* which is in contact with the psychological environment, and a central portion called the *inner-personal region.* The inner personal region is subdivided into cells which represent **tension systems.**

Psychological environment. The psychological environment consists of all those psychological factors, external to the person, that determine his behavior. The psychological environment is differentiated into bounded **regions.**

Region. A region is a differentiated portion of the life space. The two large regions are the person and the psychological environment, but each of these regions is subdivided into smaller regions. The number of regions is determined by the number of different psychological facts that exist at any given moment.

Regions are separated from one another by boundaries that act as resistances or barriers to **locomotion** or **communication.** Boundaries vary in the amount of resistance they offer to locomotions and communications between regions. Regions also have their own properties. One important property is that of *fluidity-rigidity.* A fluid region is one that responds quickly to any influence that is brought to bear on it. A rigid region resists change.

Differentiation. This is Lewin's most important developmental concept. Differentiation refers to the increase in the number of regions in the person and in the psychological environment. The number of regions increases with age, reflecting the greater psychological complexity of the adult as compared with the child.

Locomotion is the path that a person takes in moving through his psychological environment. This path is determined by the strength of the boundaries between regions, by properties of the environment, such as fluidity-rigidity, and by **vectors** and **valences.** Locomotions may be physical movements, or they may be social ones, such as joining a club, or vocational ones, such as being promoted, or intellectual ones, such as solving a problem, or any other type of mobility.

Communication. When one region within the person affects an adjacent region, the first region is said to be in communication with the second region. Communications among regions of the person are determined by the strength of the boundaries, by their closeness to each other, and by the relative amount of tension within each region.

FOREIGN HULL

The foreign hull is the portion of the nonpsychological environment that lies outside and adjacent to the boundary of the life space. It consists of the physical world and the social-cultural environment. It can and does penetrate the life space.

NEED

This is Lewin's basic motivational concept. A need may arise from a physiological condition, such as hunger, or it may be a desire for something or an intention to do something. Needs release energy, increase **tension,** and determine the strength of **vectors** and **valences.**

Tension system. A system (region) within the person is said to be in a state of tension whenever a need or intention exists. The greater the tension is, the greater is the force that is exerted on the boundary of the region.

Valence. A valence is the value a region in the psychological environment has for the person. Valences may be either positive or negative. A valence is positive when the person thinks the region can alleviate tension. A valence is negative when the person thinks the region will increase tension. A region with a positive valence induces the person to make a locomotion in its direction. A region with negative valence repels the person.

Vector. A vector is a force arising from a need that acts on the person and that determines the direction of his path through the psychological environment. Vectors are coordinated with valences. For every region endowed with a positive valence, there is a vector that pushes the person in its direction. For every region which has a negative valence, there is a vector that pushes the person away from it.

LEVEL OF ASPIRATION

The level of aspiration is defined as the difference between how a person expects or aspires to perform on a given task and how he actually does perform. Typically, a person's level of aspiration is slightly above his level of performance. If he succeeds in fulfilling his expectation, the level of aspiration rises; if he fails, the level of aspiration falls.

CONFLICT

Lewin distinguished three types of conflict. (1) A person is confronted by two positive valences of approximately equal strength. (2) A person stands between two negative valences of approximately equal strength. (3) A person is exposed to opposing forces of a positive valence and a negative valence.

GROUP DYNAMICS

This is the basic concept in Lewin's social psychology, and it has generated many investigations and applications. The concept states that the members of a group constitute a dynamic field such that change in the behavior of one member can induce a change in behavior of other members. Lewin's work in group dynamics is being carried on by the Research Center for Group Dynamics at the University of Michigan.

REFERENCES

Lewin, K. *A Dynamic Theory of Personality.* New York: McGraw-Hill, 1935.
Lewin, K. *Principles of Topological Psychology.* New York: McGraw-Hill, 1936.
Lewin, K. *Resolving Social Conflicts: Selected Papers on Group Dynamics.* Edited by Gertrude W. Lewin. New York: Harper and Row, 1948.
Lewin, K. *Field Theory in Social Science: Selected Theoretical Papers.* Edited by D. Cartwright. New York: Harper and Row, 1951.

Abraham H. Maslow

1908–1970

Maslow was a leading spokesman for humanistic psychology, which he called a "third force" in psychology, the other two forces being behaviorism and psychoanalysis. Humanistic psychology stands for a positive approach to the study of the inner nature of man, an approach that emphasizes the fullest realization of man's finest and most creative potentialities.

Abraham Harold Maslow was born in Brooklyn, New York, on April 1, 1908. All of his degrees were earned at the University of Wisconsin, where he did research on primate behavior. For fourteen years (1937–1951) he was on the faculty of Brooklyn College. In 1951, Maslow went to Brandeis University, where he remained until 1969, when he became resident fellow of the Laughlin Foundation in Menlo Park, California. Maslow suffered a fatal heart attack on June 8, 1970.

Maslow was a very articulate and persuasive writer, and his books are widely read. Many of the concepts he used were borrowed from other psychologists, but he also originated several new ones that deserve our attention. These are **metaneeds, self-actualizing persons,** and **peak experiences.**

METANEEDS

Maslow's theory of motivation contains two major concepts, basic needs and metaneeds. Basic needs are those of hunger, affection, security, self-esteem, and the like. The concept of basic needs is not original with Maslow; it has been espoused by every writer on motivation.

Metaneed is a distinctive concept. Maslow argues that man needs beauty, justice, goodness, wholeness, and order in his life just as much as he needs food, air, sex, and security. These metaneeds are growth or being needs (B-needs), whereas the basic needs are deficiency needs (D-needs). The deficiency needs ordinarily take precedence over the growth needs, and must be satisfied before a person can begin to work on fulfilling his being needs. The metaneeds are as instinctive or inherent in man as the basic needs are, and when they are not fulfilled the person is dissatisfied and unhappy, and may even become neurotic. The satisfaction of metaneeds is especially characteristic of **self-actualizing persons.**

SELF-ACTUALIZING PERSONS

Other psychologists, notably Jung (see p. 95) and Goldstein (see p. 66), developed the concept of *self-actualization,* but it was Maslow who discovered the common core of traits that distinguish self-actualizing individuals. He used the word actualizing rather than actualized because he believed it is a process of becoming or growth, not an attainable end-state.

Some of the distinguishing features of self-actualizing persons are as follows. (1) They are realistic, independent, spontaneous, creative, and democratic. (2) They are problem-centered rather than self-centered. (3) They have a need for privacy and detachment. (4) Their appreciation of people and things is fresh rather than stereotyped. (5) They resist conformity to society. Self-actualizing persons have numerous **peak experiences.**

PEAK EXPERIENCES

A peak experience is one of intense happiness and joy, of ecstasy, rapture, and bliss. Peak experiences result from profound esthetic experiences, love and passion, religious ecstasy, great achievements, creative accomplishments, and so forth. During a peak experience a person feels more whole, more alive, more at one with the world, more self-sufficient, more spontaneous and less inhibited, less aware of the passage of time, and more aware of beauty, truth, goodness, justice, simplicity, and order. Peak experiences are self-actualizing experiences.

REFERENCES

Maslow, A. H. *Toward a Psychology of Being.* Princeton, N.J.: Van Nostrand, 2d ed., 1968.

Maslow, A. H. *Motivation and Personality.* New York: Harper and Row, rev. ed., 1970.

Maslow, A. H. *The Farther Reaches of Human Nature.* New York: Viking, 1972.

William McDougall

1871–1938

The question of whether the concept of instinct is applicable to human behavior, as it is to the behavior of other species, has been a very controversial one throughout the history of psychology. In recent years, the concepts of drive and need have taken the place of the older term instinct without, however, changing the question in any essential respect. The first modern psychologist to draw up a list of human instincts was the British psychologist William McDougall.

William McDougall was born in 1871 in Lancashire, England, where his father owned a chemical firm. After attending private schools in England and Germany, McDougall entered the University of Manchester at the age of fifteen. Four years later, he enrolled at Cambridge University, from which he graduated with highest honors. McDougall was awarded a scholarship for St.

Thomas' Hospital, London, where he obtained a degree in medicine. During this time he became interested in psychology when he read William James' *Principles of Psychology* (see p. 91), and decided to prepare himself for a career in psychology. He joined a group of scientists who were doing research in the Far East, and McDougall himself undertook psychological investigations. Following this experience, he went to Germany to study experimental psychology. McDougall then accepted a position at University College, London, to teach experimental psychology. In 1904 he received an appointment at Oxford University, where he remained until the First World War began, at which time he was commissioned a major in the Medical Corps and was placed in charge of the treatment of "shell-shocked" soldiers. After the war, McDougall went through an analysis with Carl Jung (see p. 95).

In 1920 McDougall was invited to be a professor of psychology at Harvard University, a position he held until 1927, when he went to Duke University in North Carolina. Duke University was a center for parapsychology, and McDougall was very much interested in such psychic phenomena as mental telepathy and clairvoyance. He remained at Duke until his death in 1938.

McDougall was a prolific writer. He wrote 24 books and 160 articles. He often championed unpopular subjects, such as the doctrine of acquired characters (Lamarckianism), the group mind, parapsychology, teleology, and human instincts.

McDougall called himself a *hormic* psychologist. Hormic is from a Greek word which means a vital impulse or an urge to action. The basic urges or motives are the **instincts.** Associated with each instinct is an **emotion.** Any emotion can develop into a **sentiment.** Emotions can combine to form **complex emotions.**

INSTINCT AND EMOTION

These two concepts have to be treated together because each of the principal instincts is always accompanied by its own specific emotional state. An instinct is an inborn urge to behave in a certain way. The emotion associated with an instinct is also inborn. McDougall identified the following principal instincts and primary emotions, which are found in all human beings. They may be found in other species as well.

The instinct of *flight* and the emotion of *fear.* The natural tendency for all animals, including man, is to flee from danger. Flight is necessary for survival. The emotion of fear, which is aroused by perception of danger, intensifies the flight reaction.

The instinct of *repulsion* and the emotion of *disgust.* When we are disgusted, we tend to repulse or remove the object that is the cause of our disgust. A baby will spit out food that has an offensive smell or taste.

The instinct of *curiosity* and the emotion of *wonder.* When something excites a sense of wonder in us, the natural tendency is to become curious about it, and to examine it more closely. This instinct is the source of all knowledge, and it is particularly strong in childhood.

The instinct of *pugnacity* and the emotion of *anger.* Anger does not have any specific object that initially excites it. It is produced when the expression of one of the other instincts is frustrated. A child will become angry, for example, when his play is interrupted. One's immediate impulse when angry is to attack and destroy the frustrating agent. McDougall notes that when a person acquires self-control over pugnacity, the energy conserved then becomes available for the expression of other instincts.

The instinct of *subjection* and the emotion of *negative self-feeling.* By subjection McDougall means being submissive. We become submissive in order to avoid attracting attention to ourselves. We remain in the background. At the same time, we have negative feelings about ourselves.

The instinct of *self-display* and the emotion of *positive self-feeling.* This instinct is the opposite of the instinct of subjection. Self-display is a social instinct which is exhibited in the presence of spectators. It consists of all those acts that call attention to oneself. Positive self-feelings consist of feelings of delight, elation, pride, and the like.

The *parental* instinct and the *tender* emotion. The parental instinct is expressed by the rearing and protection of one's own offspring. The parental instinct is the strongest of all the instincts and takes precedence over them all because it works directly in the service of the survival of the species, whereas the other instincts work primarily in the service of individual survival. The tender emotion is weaker in men than in women.

Instincts that have no well-defined emotions associated with them are those of reproduction, gregariousness, acquisitiveness, and constructiveness.

SENTIMENT

A sentiment is an organization of feelings and attitudes that causes the person to react to an object, usually in either a positive or a negative way. A person with a patriotic sentiment, for example, has many ways of expressing his love for his country. A sentiment is formed through the repeated excitement of any one of the emotions. For instance, the sentiment of love can begin with repeated acts of tenderness expressed by one's parents. The three main sentiments are *love, hate,* and self-regard.

Self-regard. This sentiment is the most important one because of its strength and large scope. The sentiment of self-regard is the sense of the "I" or the "me"; it is consciousness of oneself. Through experience the object "me" becomes represented in the mind by a system of dispositions of great extent and complexity, and a network of associations with a multitude of past events located more or less definitely in time and place. In the normal personality, the two main tendencies of the sentiment of self-regard, those of self-assertion and submission, are nicely balanced. In this case, the sentiment is properly called *self-respect.*

COMPLEX EMOTIONS

Individual emotions can combine and fuse to form complex emotions. Complex emotional states can be divided into two groups. One group requires the presence of a sentiment, the other group does not. Jealousy, for example, requires the sentiment of love before it can exist. In order to experience sorrow, there must also first be a sentiment of love. Happiness is a complex emotion which arises when all the sentiments are working together harmoniously in pursuit of a common goal.

Complex emotions that do not imply the existence of sentiments are those of admiration, reverence, gratitude, scorn, contempt, loathing, and envy. Scorn, for example, is a mixture of disgust and anger. Loathing is a compound of disgust and fear. Reverence is a blend of wonder, fear, gratitude, and negative self-feeling.

REFERENCES

McDougall, W. *An Introduction to Social Psychology.* London: Methuen, 1908.
McDougall, W. *The Group Mind.* New York: Putnam, 1920.
McDougall, W. *An Outline of Psychology.* New York: Scribner, 1926.

Gardner Murphy

b. 1895

Gardner Murphy is an eclectic psychologist. This means he has borrowed concepts from many sources in constructing his viewpoint, which he calls a biosocial approach. Because some of these concepts have been greatly developed and elaborated by Murphy, they merit our attention.

Gardner Murphy was born in Chillicothe, Ohio, on July 8, 1895. His father was an Episcopal minister. Three prominent universities contributed to Murphy's education. Yale awarded him the B.A. degree in 1916, Harvard the M.A. in 1917, and Columbia the Ph.D. in 1923. His studies were interrupted by the First World War, when Murphy served with the American Expeditionary Forces. From 1921 to 1940 he was a member of the psychology faculty of Columbia University. In 1940, Murphy became chariman of the department of psychology of the City

College of New York, where he remained until 1952, when he was invited to become director of research at the renowned Menninger Foundation of Topeka, Kansas. In 1967 he entered upon his third professorship, at George Washington University in Washington, D.C. In awarding Murphy its Gold Medal for 1972, the American Psychological Foundation made the following citation: "A peerless teacher, a felicitous writer, an eclectic psychologist of limitless range, he seeks to bring the whole of human experience to bear in understanding behavior." Murphy's wife, Lois, is also a distinguished psychologist.

Murphy's concepts that we will discuss are **sensory needs, activity needs, canalization, perceptual learning, role,** and **situationism.**

SENSORY NEEDS

Murphy believes that the sense organs are the loci of many esthetic needs which demand to be fulfilled. The eyes need to be stimulated by beautiful scenes, the ears by harmonious sounds, the nose by fragrant odors, the mouth by delicious tastes, and the skin by pleasing contacts. These sensory needs are organic in character; they are not learned nor are they dependent on other motives.

ACTIVITY NEEDS

The muscles, tendons, and joints need to be active. Swimming, playing basketball or tennis, climbing mountains, dancing, and so forth, are pleasurable because they exercise the muscles. Such activities do not arise out of any other motives; they are the expression of needs within the muscles themselves.

CANALIZATION

Canalization is the process by which motivational energy finds an outlet in behavior. Each time the act is repeated, the channel between motive and act is deepened. For instance, a child discovers that tension can be reduced by sucking his thumb. Every time he sucks his thumb, the habit is strengthened, and eventually it becomes very difficult to break. Canalization is similar to Freud's concept of cathexis (see p. 48).

PERCEPTUAL LEARNING

Murphy points out that we not only learn to perform various acts and skills, but also learn ways of perceiving the world. These perceptual habits become deeply ingrained, and they serve to give meaning and stability to the world.

ROLE

Role is a concept employed by Murphy to describe the way in which a person becomes socialized. The socialized person is seen as playing various roles which have been defined for him in terms of his age, sex, occupation, status, and other considerations.

SITUATIONISM

Murphy believes that psychology should pay more attention to the situational determinants of behavior. He asserts that human beings respond to situations as the situations require them to respond. When the situation changes, a person's behavior also changes.

REFERENCE

Murphy, G. *Personality: A Biosocial Approach to Origins and Structures.* New York: Harper, 1947.

Henry Murray

b. 1893

Henry Murray, for many years a professor of psychology at Harvard University, developed a point of view which he called personology. The focus of this viewpoint is the study of the individual, both as a biological organism with inborn needs and as a person responsive to and shaped by the pressures of the physical and social environments.

Henry Alexander Murray was born in New York City on May 13, 1893, of well-to-do parents. Like many others who have made important contributions to psychological thought, Murray did not receive a formal education in psychology. After graduating from a private preparatory school, Groton, he went to Harvard, where he majored in history. He then enrolled in the Columbia College of Physicians and Surgeons, receiving his medical degree in 1915. For several years thereafter he was engaged in medical research, and was awarded an M.A. in biology by Columbia University and a Ph.D. in biochemistry by Cambridge University, England, in 1927.

About the same time that he received his Ph.D., his interest in psychology was aroused by reading and later visiting Carl Jung (see p. 95). Thereafter, Murray devoted himself exclusively to psychology. He became an instructor in psychology at Harvard University in 1927, and remained there, except for a interlude as director of an assessment center for the Office of Strategic Services during the Second World War, until his retirement in 1962.

For a number of years, Murray was director of the Harvard Psychological Clinic, where he conducted research on personality with the cooperation of many colleagues and students. Their joint efforts culminated in a very influential book, *Explorations in Personality* (1938). The explorations were made on a group of young men and employed a large array of clinical, psychoanalytic, experimental, physiological, and life history methods.

Murray himself, in collaboration with Christiana Morgan, devised the *Thematic Apperception Test.* This test consists of a number of black and white pictures which are shown to a subject one at a time with the instruction that he should tell a story about each picture. Such a test is called a projective test, because it is assumed the subject projects his feelings, wishes, anxieties, and other inner psychological states into the stories he tells. The analysis of the stories is based on Murray's concepts of **need** and **press.**

Murray is also a dedicated scholar of the writings of Herman Melville, and his publications in this area are highly regarded by Melville experts.

Although Murray was strongly influenced by Freudian and Jungian psychoanalysis—he was a founding member of the Boston Psychoanalytic Society—and was largely responsible for introducing psychoanalytic theory into academic psychology, he developed his own concepts of what psychology should be. Psychologists should concern themselves primarily with the study of individual lives. In studying an individual's life, Murray's strategy consists of reducing the complexities of behavior to identifiable and manageable structural units. The basic unit is called a **proceeding,** a succession of proceedings is a **serial,** a planned series is a **serial program,** and a plan for satisfying conflicting aims is a **schedule.**

Murray's motivational concepts are considered to be his most important contributions to psychological theory. These concepts are **need, press, thema,** and **unity-thema.**

PROCEEDING

A proceeding is a significant but fairly short pattern of behavior which has a recognizable beginning and end. Examples are buying something in a store, writing a letter, and baking a cake. A number of different proceedings may occur during the same period of time. For example, a person may write a letter, answer the telephone, drink a cup of coffee, pet his dog, and smoke a cigarette in a given time period. These overlapping proceedings are called a *durance.*

SERIAL

Some proceedings recur intermittently over a long period of time. Thus, a husband and wife will interact with one another intermittently throughout their marriage. These interactions constitute an organized set of proceedings to which Murray gives the name serial.

SERIAL PROGRAM

A serial program is a planned series of proceedings that lead to a remote goal, such as becoming a lawyer, a musician, or a millionaire. Each proceeding in the series has a subgoal which when reached brings the person closer to the final goal.

SCHEDULE

Often a person finds himself in conflict over whether he should engage in this proceeding or that one. He may resolve the conflict by adopting a schedule in which the competing proceedings can be accommodated. A family budget is an example of a schedule.

The family's income is allotted to a variety of proceedings (expenditures) according to a definite plan.

NEED

This concept, along with **press,** are the two most useful concepts proposed by Murray. A need stands for a force in the brain. It organizes and directs perception, memory, thought, and action in such a way as to reduce dissatisfaction and increase satisfaction. Needs may be aroused by internal states, such as hunger, or they may be set in action by external stimulation, such as the sight of food.

Murray has identified various types of needs. These are:

Primary organic needs, for instance, sex, and **secondary psychological needs,** for instance, the need for achievement;

Overt needs, which are expressed openly in behavior, and **covert needs,** which are inhibited and express themselves in thinking and daydreaming;

Focal needs, which can be satisfied by only a few goal objects, and **diffuse needs,** which can be satisfied by a wide range of goal objects;

Proactive needs, which arise from within the person, and **reactive needs,** which are aroused by stimulation from the environment;

Effect needs, which aim at reaching a goal, and **modal needs,** which involve doing something with excellence and style.

Murray has identified a number of important needs. Some of these are achievement, affiliation, aggression, deference, nurturance, and play.

PRESS

A press is a property or attribute of an object or a person which helps or hinders the efforts of an individual to reach a desired goal. Typical press are poverty, illness, loss, encouragement, and help. (Note: The plural of press is press and not presses.)

THEMA

A thema is a unit of behavior which consists of a need and a press. An illustration of a thema is a person who wants a drink of water, but is not able to find a glass. A series of themas is called a *serial thema.* Illustrative of a serial thema is playing tennis.

UNITY-THEMA

A unity-thema is a pattern of related needs and press which is repeated in various forms throughout an individual's life. A unity-thema is derived from infantile experience and operates largely unconsciously. An example is that of a person who has a strong need for order, punctuality, and accuracy.

REFERENCES

Murray, H. A. and collaborators. *Explorations in Personality.* New York: Oxford, 1938.

Murray, H. A. "Preparations for the scaffold of a comprehensive system." In S. Koch, ed., *Psychology: A Study of a Science* (New York: McGraw-Hill, 1959), III, 7–54.

Murray, H. A., and C. Kluckhohn. "Outline of a conception of personality." In C. Kluckhohn, H. A. Murray, and D. Schneider, eds., *Personality: Nature, Society, and Culture* (New York, Knopf, 2d ed., 1953), pp. 3–52.

Office of Strategic Services Assessment Staff. *Assessment of Men.* New York: Rinehart, 1948.

Charles E. Osgood
b. 1916

What does the word *mother* mean to you? How about *Communism? Male? Professor? Nixon? Modern Art? New York City?* These are questions that Osgood and his associates have been investigating for a number of years.

Charles Egerton Osgood was born in Somerville, Massachusetts, on November 20, 1916. He received his B.A. degree in 1939 from Dartmouth College and his Ph.D. from Yale in 1945. He joined the department of psychology of the University of Illinois in 1949, where he has remained. He is presently professor of psychology and director of the Institute of Communications Research.

Words, or concepts as Osgood calls them, like *mother, male,* and *modern art* have several different meanings, not only for different people, but also for the same individual. *Male* may mean strength, virility, dependability, dominance, and impulsiveness for one person, and something quite different for another person. Osgood conceives of the meaning of any given word (concept) as being multidimensional in character. The multidimensionality of meaning is represented in what Osgood calls **semantic space.** The measurement of semantic space is accomplished by using a method called the **semantic differential.**

SEMANTIC SPACE

In order to understand what is meant by semantic space, think of a box. A box is said to exist in three-dimensional space. It is so many inches long, so many inches wide, and so many inches high. Any box can be described in the three dimensions of height, width, and length.

Semantic space contains all the dimensions of meaning. Theoretically, it should be possible to locate the meaning of any concept in semantic space by determining its position along each of the dimensions of meaning just as one measures the dimensions of a box. But in order to accomplish this, it is necessary to know how many dimensions there are. Although the answer to this question is not known yet, Osgood and his associates have identified three very important and universal dimensions of meaning, using factor-analysis methods. These three dimensions are **evaluation, potency,** and **activity.**

Evaluation. Imagine a straight line, one end of which is labeled *good,* the other end *bad.* Any concept can then be located along this line, which represents the evaluative dimension. This dimension is also defined by the following pairs of adjectives: *beautiful-ugly, clean-dirty, pleasant-unpleasant,* and *happy-sad.*

Potency is a dimension that is described by the following pairs of adjectives: *large-small, strong-weak, heavy-light,* and *thick-thin.*

Activity is described by such pairs of adjectives as *fast-slow, active-passive,* and *hot-cold.*

SEMANTIC DIFFERENTIAL

The semantic differential is a method employed to measure the various dimensions of meaning of any given concept. A person is presented with a concept like *mother,* and is asked to rate it along a number of different scales, such as good-bad, weak-strong, beautiful-ugly, excitable-calm, and so forth.

REFERENCE

Osgood, C. E., G. J. Suci, and P. H. Tannenbaum. *The Measurement of Meaning.* Urbana, Ill.: University of Illinois Press, 1957.

I. P. Pavlov

1849–1936

Every century has its intellectual architects, individuals who lay the foundations for the new edifices of thought and action of that century. The two chief architects of twentieth-century psychology are Pavlov and Freud. Surely every person with a high-school education has heard of **conditioned reflexes** and psychoanalysis.

Ivan Petrovich Pavlov, the USSR's most esteemed scientist, was born in Ryazan, a city southeast of Moscow, in 1849. His father was a priest and a teacher of Greek and Latin. His mother, although the daughter of a priest, could neither read nor write. Pavlov was the eldest of ten children. He attended the theological seminary in Ryazan, but abandoned his plans for entering the priesthood when he read several books on physiology. He went to St. Petersburg (now Leningrad) to study physiology, graduating in 1875. He then enrolled at the Imperial Medicosurgical Academy, graduating in 1879. He remained at the Academy and wrote a doctoral thesis in 1883.

Upon returning from two years of study in Germany, he was appointed professor of pharmacology in the St. Petersburg Institute of Experimental Medicine in 1890. Pavlov was awarded the Nobel Prize in 1904 for his research on the physiology of digestion. At this time he began his famous work on conditioned reflexes, which was to remain his dominant interest for the rest of his long scientific life. It should be noted that Pavlov always considered the conditioned reflex to be a method for studying the brain, and not a method for studying learning behavior.

In 1924 the Soviet Academy of Sciences established an Institute of Physiology for Pavlov in a city east of Moscow. The city was renamed Pavlovo in his honor, and became one of the most prominent scientific centers in the world. Pavlov was a man of tremendous energy, vitality, and charm. He was actively engaged in research until the day of his death in 1936 at the age of eighty-seven.

CONDITIONED REFLEX

What is a conditioned reflex? Imagine the following situation. A hungry person drools, that is, saliva flows from the salivary glands in his mouth, when an appetizing plate of food is set before him. Shortly before the food is presented, a bell is rung. Let this sequence of events, bell-food-salivation, occur a number of times, and then let the bell be rung without presenting the food. The person will still salivate. Salivation to the bell without food being presented is called a conditioned reflex or conditioned response. Now let us proceed to discuss the various concepts that relate to the conditioned reflex or response.

Unconditioned stimulus is any stimulus that produces a response, for example, food.

Unconditioned response is the response that is made to the unconditioned stimulus, for example, salivation.

Conditioned stimulus is a stimulus, for example, a bell, that originally does not evoke the unconditioned response, but which, when repeatedly paired with the unconditioned stimulus, becomes able to evoke the unconditioned response.

Conditioned response is the response that is made to the conditioned stimulus. It is usually the same as or similar to the unconditioned response, for example, salivation.

Reinforcement is the strengthening of a connection between a conditioned stimulus (the bell) and the unconditioned response (salivation) by the presentation of the unconditioned stimulus (food).

Extinction is the weakening and eventual disappearance of a conditioned response when reinforcement is discontinued, that is, when food is no longer presented.

Spontaneous recovery is the reappearance of the extinguished conditioned response following an elapse of time in which there is no repetition of the conditioned stimulus. Spontaneous recovery is attributed to the weakening of **inhibition** (see below) in the cerebral cortex.

Generalization of a conditioned response refers to a conditioned response that is given to stimuli that are similar to the conditioned stimulus, or to other stimuli that are present in the conditioning situation. A dog that has been conditioned to salivate to a bell may also salivate to similar sounds. Generalization is explained by a cerebral event called **irradiation.**

Irradiation refers to the spread of excitation in one region of the cerebral cortex to adjacent areas of the cortex.

Differentiation is the complement of generalization. By reinforcing one conditioned stimulus and not reinforcing another conditioned stimulus, the conditioned response will eventually be made to the first stimulus and not to the second stimulus. In other words, the person learns to discriminate between the two stimuli. Differentiation is explained by the development of **inhibition** in the cerebral cortex.

Inhibition is one of the two basic processes in the brain, the other being *excitation*. Excitation of cells in a certain region of the cerebral cortex produces the response of salivation. Inhibition of those same cells prevents salivation. Learning to make a discrimination between two stimuli requires that one stimulus excites the cells and the other stimulus inhibits the cells.

REFERENCES

Pavlov, I. P. *Conditioned Reflexes.* London: Oxford University Press, 1927.

Pavlov, I. P. *Lectures on Conditioned Reflexes.* New York: International, 1928.

Pavlov, I. P. *Conditioned Reflexes and Psychiatry.* New York: International, 1941.

Pavlov, I. P. *Experimental Psychology and Other Essays.* New York: Philosophical Library, 1957.

Jean Piaget
b. 1896

Jean Piaget, the Swiss psychologist, is regarded as the foremost living child and educational psychologist. He has been investigating intellectual development and theorizing about his findings since the early 1920's, and is still very active. A prolific writer, Piaget's publications number in the hundreds. His early books, which established his reputation, are based on observations and experiments made by Piaget and his wife on their two daughters.

Piaget's chief interest lies in the area of intellectual or cognitive behavior as it is manifested during childhood and adolescence. In the broadest sense, he is interested in the relationships that are formed between the individual as knower and the world which he tries to know. Piaget considers himself to be a genetic epistemologist. Epistemology is the investigation of the nature and origin of knowledge, and genetic refers to development.

Jean Piaget was born in Neuchatel, Switzerland, on August 9, 1896. His mother's poor mental health was the original stimulus for his interest in psychology, although this interest was not to manifest itself professionally until after he had gained an international reputation for his scientific studies of mollusks. He published his first scientific paper at the age of ten! After receiving his Ph.D. in 1917 at the age of 21 from the University of Neuchatel for a dissertation on mollusks, he went to Zurich to work in a psychological laboratory. Not finding the work interesting there, he went to Paris, where he constructed reasoning tests for children. Out of this work grew his lifelong preoccupation with the intellectual growth of children.

In 1921, he accepted a position as director of studies at the Institut J. J. Rousseau in Geneva, where he pursued studies on the psychology of thought. In 1940, he became professor of psychology at the University of Geneva, and in 1952 professor of child psychology at the Sorbonne in Paris. He also established a Center for Genetic Epistemology.

Despite a very heavy program of writing, lecturing, and research, Piaget found time to be active in UNESCO (United Nations Educational, Scientific, and Cultural Organization) and in the educational affairs of Switzerland. He has been the recipient of numerous honors, and is regarded by many as being the greatest living psychologist.

Among the wealth of concepts that Piaget has contributed to the psychology of intellectual development, two stand out. These are the concepts of **functional invariants** and **structures.**

Functional invariants are those cognitive processes that are inborn, universal, and independent of age. The three main invariants that Piaget discusses are **accommodation, assimilation,** and **organization.**

Structures are intellectual processes that change with age. Piaget has identified the structures characteristic of the following periods of development: **period of sensory-intelligence, period of preoperational thought, period of concrete operations,** and **period of formal operations.**

FUNCTIONAL INVARIANTS

By functional invariants, Piaget means those processes that are basic and essential to intellectual functioning. They are inborn and universal, and they are independent of age. Piaget has identified three such invariants: **accommodation, assimilation,** and **organization.** Taken together they constitute what has been called the **accommodation-assimilation model** of intelligence.

Accommodation is the invariant process of adapting oneself to the requirements or demands that objects, by their nature, impose on the individual. In other words, a person must accommodate himself to the reality of the external world.

Assimilation is the process by which objects or their attributes are incorporated into the existing intellectual structures of the individual. Intellectual assimilation is analogous to the incorporation and digestion of food. There are four ways in which assimilation can occur. These are **reproductive assimilation, recognitory assimilation, generalizing assimilation,** and **reciprocal assimilation.**

Reproductive assimilation. The most primitive kind of assimilation consists of repeating the same reaction to an object or environmental situation whenever it recurs. For example, a baby may grasp an object whenever it is presented. Reproducing the same response over and over again enables the baby to become familiar with and assimilate the various features of an object or situation.

Recognitory assimilation. After becoming acquainted with a variety of objects and their attributes through reproductive assimilation, the next step is to discriminate among different objects, so that appropriate reactions can be made to them. This is called recognitory assimilation, or assimilation by recognizing differences. For example, a child learns to discriminate an object that can be grasped from one that cannot be grasped, an object that is round from one that is square, and one that is green from one that is red. Discrimination is the earliest manifestation of "thinking about" or contemplating the world.

Generalizing assimilation. After a child has acquired the ability to recognize differences among objects, he then begins to notice similarities among different objects. As a result, he can generalize that such and such objects belong to the same general class, and such and such objects belong to another general class. For example, he makes the generalization that there is a class of objects which can be and may be handled, and another generalization that there is a class of objects which cannot be or may not be handled.

Reciprocal assimilation refers to the uniting of two or more cognitive structures to form a larger totality. For instance, knowledge of an object obtained by looking at it combines with knowledge of the object obtained by feeling it. Vision and touch unite in a single organized whole.

Organization. Every intellectual or cognitive act is embedded in a larger organization. Intellectual acts are not discrete or chaotic; they are always organized. The name Piaget gives to this organization of intellectual acts is **schema.**

Schema is a cognitive plan which determines the sequence of acts that will lead to the solution of a problem. The acts may vary, but the schema remains constant. Different kinds of schemas emerge during development, but the fact that there is always some kind of schema present in intellectual functioning is an invariant condition.

Assimilation-accommodation model. The outcome of any intellectual encounter with the environment depends on the existing state of the individual and the properties of the environment. The individual can only assimilate those elements of the environment that he can accommodate himself to. Assimilation and accommodation always operate together, although at any given time one may carry more weight than the other.

A cognitive act in which assimilation and accommodation are in balance or equilibrium constitutes an *intellectual adaptation.*

The kinds of assimilations and accommodations an individual can make at any given stage of development depends on the **structures** that have been formed in him.

STRUCTURE

In order to understand Piaget's concept of structure, it is necessary to compare it with two other concepts, those of *function* and *content.* Function refers to the invariant processes of assimilation, accommodation, and organization which have already been presented. Content refers to the actual behavior of the person, and needs no further elaboration.

Structure comprises the organizing processes that intervene between the underlying invariant functions and the content of the actual behavior. Structures change with stage of development; invariant functions never do.

A number of structures have been identified for each of the four major periods of development. These periods are the **period of sensory-motor intelligence** (birth to two years), the **period of preoperational thought** (two to six years), the **period of concrete operations** (six to eleven years), and **the period of formal operations** (eleven to fifteen years).

Period of sensory-motor intelligence. The behavior of the baby at birth and for a time thereafter is reflex in character. Something stimulates a sense-organ, and an automatic motor response is made to it. By the age of two, he has learned to make fairly well-organized sensory-motor adjustments to his environment. The principal cognitive structure of this period is the **circular reaction.**

Circular reaction. A circular reaction is a simple sensory-motor adaptive response which is formed by being repeated a number of times. The first appearance of the response is a purely chance affair. Through repetition, the adaptive response becomes strengthened and firmly incorporated into the behavior repertoire of the child. For example, a child will learn to close his eyes and draw back his head when an object unexpectedly comes close to his face.

Period of preoperational thought. During this period the child acquires the ability to manipulate his environment symbolically, that is, by inner representations or thoughts about the external world. The principle cognitive structures of this period are **egocentrism, centration,** and **irreversibility.**

Egocentrism is a cognitive structure whose characteristic feature is that of seeing the world solely from a subjective or egocentric point of view. The child is not aware of being egocentric, because he is not aware that there are other points of view. Consequently, he cannot be critical, logical, or realistic in his thinking.

Centration consists of focusing attention on one feature of a situation and ignoring all other features.

Irreversibility. Faced by a problem to solve, a person starts out with an idea of the way to proceed in order to reach a solution. If he reaches an impasse, he can backtrack and start again on a new track. The preschool child is unable to do this. He cannot reverse the direction of his thinking once he has started on a solution.

Period of concrete operations. It is during this period that the child achieves a coherent and organized symbolic system of thinking, which he uses to manipulate and control his environment. Assimilation and accommodation are in balance. The main structural concept of this period is **grouping.**

Grouping consists of forming a system of classification that enables the child to recognize the members of a true logical class, for instance, a class of triangles or a class of dogs, as distinct from a mere collection of elements. By his ability to form groups, the world of diverse objects and events becomes organized and stabilized for the child. In order to achieve a system of logical groupings or categories, the child must move from egocentrism to a realistic orientation towards the world, from centering on one feature of the environment (centrism) to taking into consideration all aspects of the situation (decentration), and from irreversibility of thinking to reversibility.

Period of formal operations. The adolescent is able to go beyond the reality of the present to consider what might happen in the future. He is able to formulate hypotheses and predictions, and to test them. In other words, formal thinking is synonymous with scientific reasoning. The cognitive structure which accomplishes this is called a **lattice-group structure.**

Lattice-group structure is one which contains all the possible combinations of hypothetical propositions that can be generated regarding a future event. It is a network of ideas in which everything is related to everything else.

EQUILIBRATION PROCESS

This process consists of assimilating a new cognitive structure to an existing one without disrupting or destroying the existing structure. The equilibration process enables the individual to move smoothly from one period to the next.

REFERENCES

Battro, A. M. *Piaget: Dictionary of Terms.* Elmsford, N.Y.: Pergamon, 1973.
Beard, R. M. *An Outline of Piaget's Developmental Psychology for Students and Teachers.* New York: New American Library (Mentor), 1972.
Boyle, D. G. *A Student's Guide to Piaget.* Elmsford, N.Y.: Pergamon, 1970.
Flavell, J. H. *The Developmental Psychology of Jean Piaget.* New York: Van Nostrand, 1963.
Piaget, J. *The Language and Thought of the Child.* New York: Harcourt, Brace, 1926.
Piaget, J. *Judgment and Reasoning in the Child.* New York: Harcourt, Brace, 1928.
Piaget, J. *The Child's Conception of the World.* New York: Harcourt, Brace, 1929.
Piaget, J. *The Child's Conception of Physical Causality.* New York: Harcourt, Brace, 1930.
Piaget, J. *The Psychology of Intelligence.* New York: Harcourt, Brace, 1950.
Piaget, J. *The Origins of Intelligence in the Child.* New York: Harcourt, Brace, 1953.

Carl R. Rogers

b. 1902

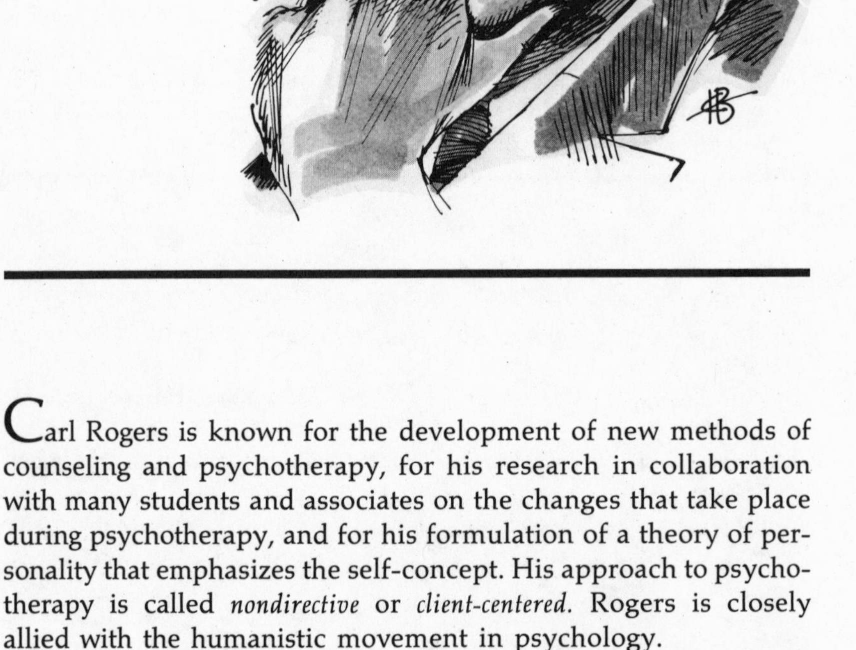

Carl Rogers is known for the development of new methods of counseling and psychotherapy, for his research in collaboration with many students and associates on the changes that take place during psychotherapy, and for his formulation of a theory of personality that emphasizes the self-concept. His approach to psychotherapy is called *nondirective* or *client-centered.* Rogers is closely allied with the humanistic movement in psychology.

Carl Ransom Rogers was born in Oak Park, Illinois, on January 8, 1902, the fourth of six children. His educational interests began early in life, for he was an avid reader long before starting school. Despite the fact that both of Rogers' parents attended college, he describes them as being rather "antiintellectual" and strongly religious. When Rogers was twelve, his parents moved to a farm west of Chicago in order to shelter their children from the evils and temptations of city life.

Upon completion of high school, Rogers enrolled at the University of Wisconsin to study scientific agriculture, but during his sophomore year he decided to go into religious education. The following year he attended a Christian Student conference in Peking, China, a trip that lasted six months. Shortly after receiving a bachelor's degree in history from the University of Wisconsin in 1924, he married and moved to New York City, where he enrolled at the Union Theological Seminary. Rogers chose this seminary because of its liberal reputation, although his father tried to persuade him to attend a more conservative seminary. During his second year in New York City, he also took psychology courses at Columbia University. The most influential course he recalls was one in clinical psychology which dealt with the problems of children. By the third year he decided to transfer to Columbia and major in clinical and educational psychology. For his doctoral dissertation, Rogers developed a test for measuring the personality adjustment of children.

Rogers' first position after receiving his Ph.D. in 1931 was at a community guidance clinic in Rochester, New York. As a result of this experience, Rogers wrote *The Clinical Treatment of the Problem Child* (1939). In 1940 Rogers was appointed as a professor at Ohio State University, where he was actively involved in professional and research activities. While at Ohio State, he wrote his very influential book *Counseling and Psychotherapy: Newer Concepts in Practice* (1942), in which the method of nondirective counseling was set forth.

In 1945 Rogers moved to the University of Chicago, where he was professor of psychology and executive secretary of the Counseling Center. While at Chicago, Rogers continued to develop his ideas on psychotherapy, and presented them in a book *Client-centered Therapy: Its Current Practice, Implications, and Theory* (1951). In 1957 Rogers became professor of psychology and psychiatry at the University of Wisconsin. He headed a research group which made an intensive, controlled study of psychotherapy with schizophrenic patients in a mental hospital.

In 1964 Rogers began a new life at the Western Behavioral Sciences Institute in La Jolla, California, where he was freed from the constrictions and limitations of university life. Rogers describes his life at the Institute as being filled with "new directions, challenging new opportunities, and professional excitement." He is presently resident fellow at the Center for Studies of the Person in La Jolla.

Rogers' initial concept is that of the **organism,** which is the locus of all experience. The totality of these experiences is called the **phenomenal field,** a portion of which becomes differentiated to form the **self.** The relationship between the organism and the self can either be one of **congruence** or of **incongruence.** Although Rogers, like Goldstein (see p. 66) and Maslow (see p. 116), believes that the organism has only one aim, to actualize itself, he does single out for special attention two needs: the need for **positive regard** and the need for **self-regard.**

ORGANISM

The organism, psychologically conceived, is the seat of all experience. Experience includes everything potentially available to awareness that is taking place within the organism at any given moment. This totality of experience constitutes the **phenomenal field.**

The organism actualizes itself along the lines laid down by heredity. It becomes more differentiated, more expanded, more autonomous, and more socialized as it matures. This forward growth of the organism can only operate successfully when the choices the organism faces are clearly perceived and adequately symbolized.

PHENOMENAL FIELD

The phenomenal field is the individual's frame of reference. How the individual behaves depends on the phenomenal field and not on external stimulating conditions. The phenomenal field is made up of both conscious (symbolized) and unconscious (unsymbolized) experiences. Experience may not be correctly symbolized, in which case the individual will behave inappropriately.

SELF

A portion of the phenomenal field gradually becomes differentiated as the self. The self is composed of perceptions of the "I" or "me" and of perceptions of how this "I" or "me" is related to others. These perceptions have values attached to them. For example, the self may be good or bad, happy or unhappy, industrious or lazy. The self is a fluid and changing process, although it is a specific and definite entity at any particular time. In addition to the self, there is an *ideal self,* which is what the person would like to be.

CONGRUENCE

When the experiences that constitute the self faithfully reflect the experiences of the organism, the relationship between the self and the organism is a congruent one. The aim of psychotherapy is to bring about congruence between self and organism. When this is accomplished, the person is said to be functioning to his fullest extent. Such a person is open to new experiences, lacking in defensiveness, capable of viewing the world and himself realistically, and enjoys harmonious relations with others. He does not feel tense or anxious.

INCONGRUENCE

This condition is, of course, the opposite of congruence. The self-system is at odds with the organism. Since the organism is the "true" reality, incongruence necessarily means that the self-concept is a distorted one. How does the self become distorted? Largely as a result of accepting uncritically the evaluations of others. A person denies his true feelings in the face of contrary evaluations by others. The state of incongruence is one of confusion, tension, anxiety, maladjustment, vulnerability, defensiveness, and threat. Incongruence also affects adversely a person's relations with others.

Incongruence can be reduced by placing the person in the nonthreatening situation of client-centered therapy, where he can examine his true feelings in the presence of a warm, accepting counselor. The essence of psychotherapy, Rogers contends, is that the person becomes what he organismically is.

POSITIVE REGARD

The need to be positively regarded or liked by others originates during infancy as a consequence of the attention and affection a baby receives. This need can cause trouble, however, if a person acts, not in accordance with his true feelings, but in a way to please others and gain their approval. But if the positive regard is *unconditional,* that is, if there is no disapproval and negative evaluation, then no incongruity between the self and the organism would develop. The nondirective counselor maintains an attitude of unconditional positive regard toward his clients.

SELF-REGARD

Self-regard is to think well of oneself, to feel worthwhile. A person thinks well of himself when his organismic experiences are being enhanced and actualized. He also thinks well of himself when the self and the ideal-self are not too far apart. Self-regard, in the first instance, is dependent on receiving positive regard from others. But eventually it must become independent of what others think, and dependent solely on one's own values. Otherwise, incongruity between self and organism may develop, and the person cannot be what he is.

REFERENCES

Rogers, C. R. *The Clinical Treatment of the Problem Child.* Boston: Houghton Mifflin, 1939.

Rogers, C. R. *Counseling and Psychotherapy: Newer Concepts in Practice.* Boston: Houghton Mifflin, 1942.

Rogers, C. R. *Client-centered Therapy: Its Current Practice, Implications, and Theory.* Boston: Houghton Mifflin, 1951.

Rogers, C. R. "A theory of therapy, personality, and interpersonal relationships, as developed in the client-centered framework." In S. Koch, ed., *Psychology: A Study of a Science.* (New York: McGraw-Hill, 1959), III, 184–256.

Rogers, C. R. *On Becoming a Person.* Boston: Houghton Mifflin, 1961.

Rogers, C. R., ed. *The Therapeutic Relationship and Its Impact: A Study of Psychotherapy with Schizophrenics.* Madison, Wisconsin: University of Wisconsin Press, 1967.

William H. Sheldon

b. 1898

The attempt to discover dependable relationships between physique and personality has had a very long history. The most recent, and for many psychologists the most successful in its accomplishment, is the work of William H. Sheldon. Sheldon is now considered to be the leader in this field, which he calls constitutional psychology, and his concepts have become very familiar and have stimulated a lot of research.

William Herbert Sheldon was born in Warwick, Rhode Island on November 19, 1898, where he grew up in a farm setting. The rural atmosphere of his childhood has had a lasting effect on his values and on his view of human behavior. Sheldon was educated in public schools and attended Brown University, where he received his A.B. in 1919. Subsequently he received a master's degree from the University of Colorado and a Ph.D. in psychology from the University of Chicago in 1925. After teaching in several universities, Sheldon enrolled in the Medical School of the University of Chicago and obtained his M.D. in 1933.

Sheldon interned at a children's hospital, and then was awarded a fellowship to engage in psychiatric study for two years in Europe. He visited Freud and Ernst Kretschmer, the foremost investigator of the connection between body type and mental disease, but most of his time abroad was spent with Carl Jung in Zurich. On his return to the United States in 1936, Sheldon became professor of psychology at the University of Chicago. Two years later, he moved to Harvard University, where he collaborated with S. S. Stevens, the distinguished experimental psychologist. After serving for a time in the Army, Sheldon accepted a position as Director of the Constitution Laboratory, College of Physicians and Surgeons, Columbia University, where he remained until 1959. Here Sheldon was actively engaged in studying the relation between organic diseases and physical structure. He then became associated with the University of Oregon Medical School, from which he retired in 1970.

Sheldon's concepts developed out of his extensive studies of physical structure and temperament traits. After carefully examining standardized photographs of thousands of naked young men, Sheldon concluded that variations in physique could be accounted for by three primary components. These he called **endomorphy, mesomorphy,** and **ectomorphy.** Each of these components can be rated on a seven-point scale, in which 1 represents the absolute minimum of the component and 7 the absolute maximum. The three ratings represent an individual's body type or *somatotype.* For example, an individual with a 4-6-1 somatotype is about average in endomorphy, very high in mesomorphy, and almost totally lacking in ectomorphy.

Sheldon also discovered three secondary physical components. These are **dysplasia, gynandromorphy,** and **textural aspect.**

After establishing that there are three primary physical components, Sheldon then proceeded to determine the components of temperament (personality) using ratings of behavior. A statistical analysis revealed three major clusters of traits. These three primary components of temperament are called **viscerotonia, somatotonia,** and **cerebrotonia.** The magnitude of each of these components in an individual is expressed by a rating from 1 to 7. This is his *temperamental type.*

Sheldon then found that somatotype and temperamental type were fairly closely associated. That is, a person with a somatotype of 4-6-1 tends to be of a 4-6-1 temperamental type.

PRIMARY COMPONENTS OF PHYSIQUE

Endomorphy. This component consists of softness, a spherical appearance, an underdevelopment of bone and muscle, and a relatively low surface-mass ratio. A person who is high in this component and low in the other two is a "fatty." The fact that the digestive organs are highly developed in this physique and that the functional elements of these organs develop primarily from the endodermal embryonic layer accounts for the use of the term endomorphy.

Mesomorphy. This component consists of strength, hardness, and toughness, with a predominance of bone and muscle. A person who is high in this component and low in the other two is equipped for strenuous and exacting physical demands. The features of this component are derived from the mesodermal embryonic layer, hence the term mesomorphy.

Ectomorphy. Thinness, light muscles, flatchestedness, and fragility are characteristics of this component. A person high in this component and low in the other two is skinny. He also has the largest brain and central nervous system in proportion to his size. These organs are derived from the ectodermal embryonic layer, thus the name ectomorphy.

SECONDARY COMPONENTS OF PHYSIQUE

Dysplasia. Dysplasia is the term used when the physique is inconsistent or uneven with respect to the three primary components, for example, when the torso is mesomorphic and the legs are ectomorphic.

Gynandromorphy. This represents the extent to which the physique possesses characteristics ordinarily associated with the opposite sex. A male who is high in this component is characterized by a soft body, a broad pelvis, and wide hips, as well as other feminine features, including long eyelashes and small facial features.

Textural aspect. This term refers to the coarseness or fineness of the physical texture. A person high in this component, that is, who has fine hair, fine features, and a fine skin, is esthetically pleasing in appearance.

PRIMARY COMPONENTS OF TEMPERAMENT

Viscerotonia. An individual high in this component is characterized by love of comfort and sociability, and by strong needs for food, people, and affection. He is relaxed in posture, reacts slowly, and is even-tempered, tolerant, and easy to get along with.

Somatotonia. A high score on this component is associated with love of physical adventure and risk-taking, and a strong need for muscular and vigorous physical activity. Such a person is aggressive, dominant, callous toward the feelings of others, overmature in appearance, courageous, and noisy.

Cerebrotonia. A high score on this component implies restraint, inhibition, and the desire for concealment. This individual is secretive, self-conscious, youthful in appearance, and afraid of people, and prefers to be in small enclosed areas. He reacts quickly, sleeps poorly, and prefers solitude. He tries to avoid attracting attention to himself.

REFERENCES

Sheldon, W. H. (with the collaboration of S. S. Stevens and W. B. Tucker). *The Varieties of Human Physique: An Introduction to Constitutional Psychology.* New York: Harper, 1940.

Sheldon, W. H. (with the collaboration of S. S. Stevens). *The Varieties of Temperament: A Psychology of Constitutional Differences.* New York: Harper, 1942.

Sheldon, W. H. (with the collaboration of C. W. Dupertuis and E. McDermott). *Atlas of Men: A Guide for Somatotyping the Adult Male at All Ages.* New York: Harper, 1954.

B. F. Skinner

b. 1904

B. F. Skinner is easily the most prestigious and certainly the most controversial living American psychologist. For forty years, he has been doing experimental work in the laboratory and writing continuously about his findings and their practical implications.

Skinner is the purest example of an objective behavioristic psychologist in the tradition of Pavlov (see p. 135), Watson (see p. 177), and Thorndike (see p. 168). Unlike the neobehaviorist Hull (see p. 85) and the purposive behaviorist Tolman (see p. 172), Skinner considers speculations about what intervenes between stimulus and response or between response and reward superfluous. He is chiefly concerned with the question of how behavior can be regulated by the manipulation of rewards.

Burrhus Frederic Skinner was born in Susquehanna, Pennsylvania, on March 20, 1904. (There was another son, several years younger than Skinner, but he died before reaching maturity.) His father was a lawyer and hoped that his son would follow in his footsteps. Skinner, however, was determined to become a writer. To this end, he majored in literature at Hamilton College, a small liberal arts school in Clinton, New York. After receiving his A.B. in 1926, he spent several years writing, but the results were not productive because, he later confessed, "I had nothing important to say" (1967, p. 395).

Believing himself to be a failure as a writer, he decided to study psychology because he had always been interested in animal and human behavior. Entering Harvard, he found there a diversified and stimulating group of professors and students. He was especially influenced by the experimental biologist W. J. Crozier, and worked in his laboratory for five years after receiving his Ph.D. in 1931.

His first academic position was at the University of Minnesota. There he wrote his first and probably most important book, *The Behavior of Organisms* (1938), and began his novel *Walden Two* (1948), which is a blueprint for a utopia based on behavioristic principles. After three years as chairman of the department of psychology at Indiana University, he was offered a professorship at Harvard, where he has remained.

Despite his distaste for speculations about what goes on in the body or in the mind, Skinner is a very broad-gauge psychologist. His writings display a wide range of interests, covering such diverse topics as learning (Skinner's favorite experimental animal is the pigeon, which first came to his attention when one landed on a window ledge outside his Minnesota laboratory), verbal behavior, raising babies in a "baby box" (he and his wife raised their second child in one), the effects of drugs on behavior, teaching machines, behavior therapy, the guiding of missiles by pigeons, the design of cultures, the "automatic" writing of Gertrude Stein (she also studied psychology at Harvard), and much, much more.

In a recent book, *Beyond Freedom and Dignity* (1971), Skinner makes a number of suggestions regarding the design of a society in which the behavior of its citizens would be shaped and controlled by planned systems of rewards (reinforcements). The book was greeted with a storm of criticism and some praise. Not the least of Skinner's merits is his talent for writing clear, interesting, and engaging prose.

Although Skinner advances very few concepts, and those few are derived from Pavlov, Watson, and particularly Thorndike, he has made them extremely powerful ones. He distinguishes between two types of behavior, **respondent** and **operant,** and he shows how various **contingencies of reinforcement** can be employed to modify or control any kind of behavior.

RESPONDENT BEHAVIOR

This type of behavior is observed by presenting a stimulus to an organism and observing what response is made to it. Pavlov, Watson, Hull, and Tolman studied respondent behavior. It does not interest Skinner as much as **operant behavior** does.

OPERANT BEHAVIOR

There are many activities, like writing a story, building a house, or solving a puzzle, that do not appear to be connected with any identifiable stimulus. Skinner calls such behavior operant because it operates on and changes the environment in some manner. It is also called *instrumental* behavior because it is instrumental for achieving some goal desired by the individual.

Skinner's investigations have been concerned almost exclusively with operant behavior. Here is a typical experimental example. A hungry pigeon is placed in a cage which has a lever projecting from one of the sides. When the lever is pressed by the pigeon (an operant response), a piece of grain is automatically released into the cage from a storage bin. When the pigeon is first placed in the cage, it acts in a more or less random manner, until by chance, it hits the lever. The appearance of food and the eating of it constitutes a **reinforcement.**

REINFORCEMENT

A reinforcement is anything that changes the probability of a response being made. In the foregoing pigeon example, the probability that the lever will be pressed more quickly when the pigeon is returned to the cage is increased because that act was positively reinforced. Had the pigeon been shocked for pressing the lever, the probability of its repeating the response would have been lowered.

Skinner is not content, however, to wait for the desired operant response to be made. Learning can be speeded up by **shaping behavior.**

Shaping behavior. Suppose the task set for the pigeon is to peck at a lighted disk in the cage. The chances of the pigeon doing this spontaneously or by chance are very slim. Shaping its behavior consists of reinforcing successive approximations to the disk-pecking response. First, the bird is trained to eat from an open food bin in the cage. Then food is given to the pigeon when it goes near the disk. The next step consists of presenting food when the bird raises its head while standing near the disk. Then it is reinforced when its beak is within striking distance of the disk, and finally it is fed when it pecks the disk. This is the model for the shaping of behavior, whether it be in the laboratory, the home, school, or at work.

The rate at which the operant response, for example, pecking, is made and its persistence after the reinforcement is discontinued are affected by the **contingencies** (schedules) **of reinforcement** employed.

Contingencies of reinforcement. Reinforcement is not a new concept; it was introduced into psychology by Thorndike and Pavlov. Skinner has, however, developed the concept of contingencies of reinforcement.

Contingency refers to the conditions under which reinforcements are given. These contingencies may be arranged in the laboratory according to a deliberate schedule. In everyday life, the contingencies are more haphazard. For instance, the same act may be positively reinforced (rewarded) on some occasions and negatively reinforced (punished) on other occasions. Or the reinforcement may be given immediately following the act or it may be delayed for a long time. Since the occurrences of positive and negative reinforcements in everyday life are inevitable as well as being often haphazard, Skinner believes they should be planned and managed in order to produce the maximum advantages to the individual and to society instead of being left to chance. That is the argument set forth in his book *Beyond Freedom and Dignity.*

Three typical schedules of reinforcement used in the laboratory are **continuous reinforcement, interval reinforcement,** and **ratio reinforcement.**

Continuous reinforcement consists of giving a reward every time the desired response is made. The response quickly ceases when the reward is no longer given.

Interval reinforcement consists of giving the reward at intervals of time. These intervals may be fixed, for instance, every five minutes, in which case the pigeon learns to peck the disk or press the lever at approximately five-minute intervals. The intervals may also be made to vary in an unpredictable way, in which case the pigeon keeps up a steady rate of pecking. In the latter case, when the food reward is no longer given, pecking persists for a longer time than when it is continuously reinforced.

Ratio reinforcement consists of giving the reward after so many responses are made. The pigeon is given food after every ten pecks, for example. Or the number of times it must make a pecking response may be varied so that sometimes it is three, sometimes seven, sometimes ten pecks, and so forth. The more times the pigeon has to peck before receiving food, the more rapidly it pecks. The rate of extinction of the response following cessation of ratio reinforcement is slower than for interval reinforcement.

REFERENCES

Skinner, B. F. *The Behavior of Organisms.* New York: Appleton-Century-Crofts, 1938.

Skinner, B. F. *Walden Two.* New York: Macmillan, 1948.

Skinner, B. F. *Science and Human Behavior.* New York: Macmillan, 1953.

Skinner, B. F. "Autobiography." In E. G. Boring and G. Lindzey eds., *A History of Psychology in Autobiography* (New York: Appleton-Century-Crofts, 1967), V, 387–413.

Skinner, B. F. *Beyond Freedom and Dignity.* New York: Knopf, 1971.

Skinner, B. F. *Cumulative Record: A Selection of Papers.* New York: Appleton-Century-Crofts, 3d ed., 1972.

Skinner, B. F. *About Behaviorism.* New York: Knopf, 1974.

S. S. Stevens
1906–1973

It is customary to say that scientific psychology was born in 1860, when a German physicist and philosopher, Gustav Fechner, announced the discovery of a lawful mathematical relationship between the intensity of a physical stimulus (sound waves, for example) and the intensity of a mental sensation (a heard sound, for example). This was the first clearcut demonstration that an element of the mind (sensation) could be measured. Fechner called the new science which investigates the relationships between sensation intensities and stimulus intensities *psychophysics.* A prominent leader in contemporary psychophysics until his recent death was the Harvard psychologist, S. S. Stevens.

Stanley Smith Stevens was born in Ogden, Utah, on November 4, 1906. After serving for three years as a Mormon missionary in Europe, Stevens enrolled at the University of Utah and then transferred to Stanford, where he received his A.B. in 1931. Following graduation, he entered Harvard Medical School, but his interest in medicine waned and he shifted to psychology. His Ph.D. was awarded in 1933. Stevens remained at Harvard until his death on January 18, 1973.

According to Fechner's formulation, the relation between stimulus intensity and sensation intensity is a logarithmic one. The intensity of a sensation grows as the logarithm of stimulus intensity. Stevens showed, however, that sensation increases in intensity as a power function of stimulus intensity. This is known as the **power law.**

POWER LAW

A power function is represented by the equation $x = y^n$, in which n is an exponent. If we let x stand for the intensity of one's subjective experience (sensation) and y stand for the intensity of the physical stimulus that is producing the sensation, then we have a mathematical description of Steven's power law. The equation is x (sensation intensity) $=$ y (stimulus intensity)^n.

Once the mathematical equation has been established, the experimental task is to determine for each kind of stimulus what the exponent (n) is. That is what Stevens and his associates have done. For example, they found the exponent for judging the length of a line is 1. Thus, if a line is doubled in length, it also appears subjectively to be twice as long; so here there is a one-to-one relationship. The exponent for brightness of a light is .33 or less than 1. This means that as a light is increased in brightness, the experience of brightness does not increase as rapidly. For example, if the light intensity is increased by ten units, the apparent brightness increases only by a few units (except at very low levels of brightness). By contrast, the exponent for electric shock applied to the fingers is very high, 3.5. This means that a slight increase in the magnitude of the current produces a large increase in the shock sensation (except at low levels of shock). In other words, a person is more sensitive to an increase in shock than he is to an increase in brightness.

The power function is of theoretical importance because it calls attention to the distinctive properties of the different sense organs, which act as *transducers.* A transducer transforms the energy of an external stimulus (light waves, for instance) in such a way that a mental experience results. For example, since the exponent for a cold object placed on the arm is 1, and the exponent for a warm object is 1.6, the sense organs that are aroused by cold and warmth must have different properties.

REFERENCE

Stevens, S. S. "The psychophysics of sensory function." In W. A. Rosenblith, ed., *Sensory Communication* (Cambridge, Mass.: The M.I.T. Press, 1961).

Harry Stack Sullivan

1892–1949

Sullivan created a new psychological viewpoint which is known as the *interpersonal theory of psychiatry.* The key word is "interpersonal." All distinctively human behavior involves interactions among people. Consequently, the unit of study in psychology is the interpersonal situation and not the person.

Harry Stack Sullivan was born on a farm near Norwich, New York, on February 21, 1892. He received his medical degree from the Chicago College of Medicine and Surgery in 1917, and served with the armed forces during the First World War. In 1922 Sullivan went to Saint Elizabeth's Hospital in Washington, D.C., where he came under the influence of William Alanson White, a leader in American neuropsychiatry. From 1923 until the early thirties, he was associated with the Medical School of the University of Maryland and with the Sheppard and Enoch Pratt Hospital in

Towson, Maryland. It was during this period of his life that Sullivan conducted investigations of schizophrenia which established his reputation as a clinician. He left Maryland to open an office on Park Avenue in New York City for the express purpose of studying obsessive patients. At this time he began his formal training in psychoanalysis. In 1933 he became president of the William Alanson White Foundation, and in 1936 he helped found the Washington School of Psychiatry, which is the training institution of the Foundation. By the mid-1930's Sullivan had pretty well formulated his theory of interpersonal relations. His thinking was deeply influenced by sociologists and anthropologists, especially by the anthropologist Edward Sapir, who advocated a close working relationship between anthropology and psychoanalysis. Sullivan died on January 14, 1949 in Paris, France, on his way home from a meeting of the executive board of the World Federation for Mental Health.

Sullivan's chief concepts are those of **dynamism,** the **self-system, personification,** the cognitive processes of **prototaxis, parataxis,** and **syntaxis, anxiety,** and **energy transformation.**

DYNAMISM

A dynamism is the smallest unit of behavior that can be employed in the study of an individual. It is defined as any form of mental or physical activity which is characteristic of a person. A dynamism is much like a habit or a trait. All persons have the same basic dynamisms, although there are individual differences in the way they are expressed. The dynamisms that are distinctively human are those that involve interpersonal relations.

Most dynamisms serve the purpose of satisfying the basic needs of the organism. There is one important dynamism, however, which develops as a result of **anxiety.** This is called the dynamism of the self or the **self-system.**

Self-system. The self-system consists of a set of security measures or defenses against anxiety. These security measures sanction certain forms of behavior that conform to the "good-me-self" and forbid other forms of behavior that conform to the "bad-me-self". Although the self-system serves the useful purpose of reducing anxiety, it interferes with one's ability to live constructively with others. Sullivan believed that the self-system is a product of the irrational aspects of society. By this he meant that the young child is made to feel anxious for reasons that would not exist in a more rational society, so that he is forced to learn unnatural ways of behaving. The self-system is a stumbling block in the path of healthy personality development.

PERSONIFICATION

A personification is an image that an individual has of himself or of another person. For example, the baby develops a personification of a good mother by being cared for by her, and he builds up a personification of a bad mother when she makes the baby feel anxious. Personifications, once formed, tend to persist and to influence one's feelings about other people. Personifications are rarely accurate descriptions of the people to whom they refer.

Personifications that are shared by a number of people are called *stereotypes.* An example of a stereotype is the absent-minded professor.

PROTOTAXIS

Prototaxis is the first mode of experiencing. It refers to the flow of sensations, images, and feelings that are not connected and that have no meaning for the person. The prototaxis mode is found in its purest form during the first year of life.

PARATAXIS

The parataxic mode of thinking consists of seeing causal relationships between events that occur at about the same time but which are not logically related. Sullivan thought that much of our thinking does not advance beyond the level of parataxis.

SYNTAXIS

The syntaxic mode produces logical order among experiences and enables people to communicate with one another using symbols like words and numbers.

ANXIETY

Anxiety is the experience of tension that results from real or imaginary threats to one's security. In large amounts, it reduces the efficiency of a person; in lesser amounts, it can be informative. Anxiety is transmitted to the infant by the mother who is herself expressing anxiety through her facial expressions, tone of voice, and so forth. Sullivan said that one of the chief tasks of psychology is to study the basic vulnerabilities to anxiety in interpersonal relations.

ENERGY TRANSFORMATION

Energy is transformed into mental and physical acts. These transformations are to a great extent conditioned by the society in which the individual is raised. In growing up, an individual undergoes a number of transformations. One such transformation that many children experience Sullivan called the *malevolent transformation.* The child develops the feeling that he lives in a hostile environment and that people are his enemies. During preadolescence, an important transformation is from the family members to an intimate friend. In adolescence, there is a transformation to erotic heterosexual relations. During late adolescence there is a prolonged initiation into the privileges, duties, satisfactions, and responsibilities of social living and citizenship. When the individual has reached adulthood, he has been transformed from an animal organism into a human person, largely by means of his interpersonal relations.

REFERENCES

Sullivan, H. S. *The Interpersonal Theory of Psychiatry.* New York: Norton, 1953.

Sullivan, H. S. *The Fusion of Psychiatry and Social Science.* New York: Norton, 1964.

E. L. Thorndike

1874–1949

The topic of learning has always been a dominant one in American psychology. This interest in how we learn stems, in part, from the traditional American credo that character and intelligence are formed more by education and training than by native endowment. The question of how learning occurs, as phrased in stimulus-response language, is "How does a connection between a stimulus and a response become established?" How does a child learn, for example, to say cat when he sees a cat? Answers to this question have been given by Guthrie (see p. 71), Hull (see p. 85), Pavlov (see p. 135), Skinner (see p. 156), Tolman (see p. 172), and Watson (see p. 177). One of the earliest answers to the question was formulated by E. L. Thorndike in 1898 on the basis of his studies of animal learning. This was some years before Pavlov and

Watson appeared on the psychological scene. Thorndike's formulation is known as the **law of effect,** easily the most famous and persistent concept in the history of learning theory.

Edward Lee Thorndike was born in Williamsburg, Massachusetts, on August 31, 1874. His father was a lawyer, and later a clergyman. Thorndike entered Wesleyan University in Middletown, Connecticut, in 1891, graduating in 1895. He writes in his autobiography that he had no memory of having "heard or seen the word psychology until my junior year," when he had to take a required course in the subject. Psychology did not interest him until he read William James' *Principles of Psychology,* and then he decided to go to Harvard to study with James. At Harvard he earned another bachelor's degree in 1896 and a master's degree in 1897. James was no longer involved with experimental psychology, but he provided Thorndike with space in the basement of his home to carry out experiments with animals. Thorndike decided, however, that he would have better facilities for research elsewhere, and when he was offered a fellowship at Columbia University he went there. It was at Columbia that he completed his famous research on cats' learning to get out of a locked cage by pulling on a piece of rope, for which he was awarded the Ph.D. in 1898. Except for a year spent as an instructor at Western Reserve University in Cleveland, Ohio, the rest of his very productive life was spent at Teachers College of Columbia University. During his academic life, Thorndike wrote more than 500 articles, monographs, and books, a record of achievement which no subsequent psychologist, with the possible exception of Jean Piaget (see p. 139), has equalled.

Although we shall be mainly concerned with Thorndike's learning concepts, it should be noted that Thorndike made important contributions to many areas of psychology. He developed psychological tests which were widely used and a theory of intelligence; he studied individual and sex differences, fatigue, interests and attitudes, and vocabulary; and he wrote leading textbooks in educational psychology and texts for children. Thorndike was the most influential educational psychologist of his times.

This richly productive life came to an end on August 9, 1949, a few weeks before Thorndike's seventy-fifth birthday.

LAW OF EFFECT

In its original form, the law of effect stated that a connection between a stimulus and a response is strengthened when it is accompanied or closely followed by a satisfying state of affairs, and a connection is weakened when it is accompanied or closely followed by an annoying state of affairs. A cat learns to pull on the rope because doing so opens a door and allows the hungry cat to get food which is outside the cage. It quits making other responses because they do not lead to food.

A satisfying state of affairs is defined as one that the individual does nothing to avoid, often behaving in such a way as to continue it or to reinstate it. An annoying state of affairs is defined as something an individual does nothing to preserve, often acting in such a way as to put an end to it. A satisfying state of affairs is equivalent to a reward or a positive reinforcement. An annoying state of affairs is equivalent to a punishment or a negative reinforcement.

Later, as a result of new experimental findings, Thorndike modified the law by minimizing the effects of punishment on weakening a connection.

Spread of effect. A reward not only acts on the connection between a stimulus and a response, but also acts to strengthen connections before and after the rewarded connection. For example, if a child is learning the definitions of a list of five words, and he is only rewarded (approved) for giving the definition of the third word, the reward will also strengthen the connections between whatever definitions, right or wrong, he may have given to the preceding and following two words. This is known as the spread of effect.

BELONGINGNESS

As a partial concession to Gestalt psychology (see p. 57) and as a result of his own experiments, Thorndike formulated the concept of belongingness. This concept states that a connection is more quickly formed if the stimulus and the response appear to belong together. Thus, chair is more easily associated with table than it is with bird or sky because chair seems to belong to table and not to bird or sky.

POLARITY

Thorndike also pointed out that connections are more easily formed in the forward than in the backward direction. This is known as the concept of polarity. For example, if an English-speaking person learns Spanish, it is easier for him to give the Spanish equivalent of an English word than to give the English equivalent of a Spanish word.

TRANSFER OF IDENTICAL ELEMENTS

For many years, a controversy existed in educational circles concerning the carry-over of what a child learns in school to his activities outside of school. One view is that if a child's mind is strengthened by learning difficult subjects, such as Latin and mathematics, he will be able to deal more successfully with practical problems than if he learns easy subjects.

Thorndike opposed this view of mental discipline. He believed that specific connections between stimuli and responses are learned, and that in order for the connections learned in school to carry over to non-school situations, the connections would have to be identical. This is known as the theory of identical elements.

Thorndike's conception of intelligence was also based on the formation of specific stimulus-response connections. The larger the number of connections that a person has learned, the more intelligent he is.

REFERENCES

Thorndike, E. L. *Animal Intelligence.* New York: Macmillan, 1911.

Thorndike, E. L. *The Fundamentals of Learning.* New York: Teachers College, 1932.

Thorndike, E. L. *Human Nature and the Social Order.* New York: Macmillan, 1940.

Thorndike, E. L. *Selected Writings from a Connectionist's Psychology.* New York: Appleton-Century-Crofts, 1949.

Edward C. Tolman

1886–1959

Watson's behaviorism (see p. 177) had an enormous impact on American psychology, although it was subjected to considerable elaboration and modification by subsequent theoretical psychologists. One of the more radical modifications of classical behaviorism was made by Edward C. Tolman. Dissatisfied with Watson's stimulus-response analysis of behavior because he considered it too atomistic, Tolman argued that complex psychological processes within the organism intervene between stimulus and response. These processes, and not stimuli, are the actual determiners of behavior. The intervening processes or variables that Tolman emphasized are cognitive and purposive in nature. Tolman called his theory *Purposive Behaviorism.* Tolman considered himself to be a behaviorist, despite his opposition to Watson, because "the only psychological statements that can be scientifically validated are statements about the organism's behavior, about stimulus situations, or about inferred, but objectively definable, intervening variables" (1952, p. 331).

Edward Chace Tolman was born in West Newton, Massachusetts, on April 14, 1886, and attended public schools there. His father, a prosperous factory owner, encouraged his son to enroll at the Massachusetts Institute of Technology, from which the father had graduated and of which he was then a trustee, to prepare himself to enter the family business. After Tolman obtained a degree in electrochemistry in 1911, he rebelled against his father's plans for him, and entered Harvard University to study philosophy and psychology. He was awarded the doctorate in 1915. After serving for three years as a psychology instructor at Northwestern University, Tolman accepted an appointment at the University of California, Berkeley, where he was to remain until his retirement in 1954.

During the 1950's, when the tides of political repression were running high, Tolman was fired from his professorship because he refused to sign a loyalty oath. He led a successful fight against the oath, and he and other faculty members were reinstated in their positions by an order of the Supreme Court of California.

Soon after going to Berkeley in 1919, Tolman established a rat laboratory which was to be the scene of his experimental investigations and those of his many students throughout his long career. In gratitude to his docile, hardworking animal subjects, he dedicated his major book *Purposive Behavior in Animals and Men* (1932) to *Mus norvegicus albinus*—the scientific name for the tame white rat—whose behavior in mazes provided Tolman with the empirical sustenance for his theorizing.

Tolman was influenced not only by Watson's behaviorism, which he had studied as a graduate student at Harvard, but also by Gestalt psychology (see p. 57), Kurt Lewin (see p. 110), and Egon Brunswik (see p. 28). Despite these influences, Tolman's theory and its concepts were uniquely his own.

Tolman received every honor his professional colleagues could bestow. During the 1930's and 1940's, he and Clark Hull (see p. 85) were the two leading theorists in American psychology, and the influence of their theories is still great. Both were behaviorists, but very different kinds of behaviorists. Tolman died on November 19, 1959.

The variables that intervene between stimulus and response Tolman called **behavior determinants,** of which there are three classes, **capacities, behavior-adjustments,** and **immanent determinants.** The important immanent determinants are those of **purpose** and **cognition.** Cognitions are divided into **means-end-readinesses** and **sign-gestalt-expectations.**

Features of the environment provide opportunities for learning. These features are called **behavior supports.** There are three kinds of behavior supports: **discriminanda, manipulanda,** and **means-end-relations.**

Another important concept in Tolman's system is that of **latent learning.**

BEHAVIOR DETERMINANTS

Behavior determinants are processes or variables that intervene between the **initiating causes of behavior** and the final resulting behavior. There are three classes of behavior determinants: **capacities, behavior-adjustments,** and **immanent determinants.**

Initiating causes of behavior. There are four initiating or independent causes of behavior: (a) heredity, (b) past training, (c) present environmental stimuli, and (d) present physiological states.

Capacities are the present talents, skills, capabilities, and aptitudes of the individual. They are the product of his innate endowment and his past experience.

Behavior-adjustments. A behavior adjustment is the mental activity that occurs when an individual is confronted by a problem. It is a kind of mental running back and forth among various alternatives and options as to how the problem might be dealt with effectively. Behavior-adjustments are also called *vicarious trial-and-error.*

Immanent determinants. This is one of the central concepts in Tolman's system. An immanent determinant is a determinant of behavior that has to be inferred from variations in behavior in experimentally controlled situations. It cannot be objectively observed. There are two basic kinds of immanent determinants: **purposes** (also called demands) and **cognitions.**

Purpose. A purpose is an inborn or acquired urge to approach or to avoid a goal-object in order to reduce a physiological state of tension. A purpose is testified to objectively by persistent behavior to try to reach or to avoid a goal-object, and by the docility or modifiability of the behavior in order to deal more effectively with a problem situation. For example, a hungry organism will persist in trying to obtain food, and it will learn more efficient ways of getting food on repeated occasions.

Cognition. A cognition is an inborn or acquired readiness to behave in a certain way in a problem situation, and an expectation that such behavior will enable the organism to achieve its purpose. If the environment proves not to be what the individual is ready for or expects, his behavior will be disrupted and new learning will take place. There are two kinds of cognitions: **means-end-readiness** and **sign-gestalt-expectation.**

Means-end-readiness. A means-end-readiness is a belief held by an individual that if he acts in a certain manner he will reach a desired goal or avoid an undesired state of affairs. A means-end-readiness is initiated by a demand, and it is guided by innate endowment and by past experience. A means-end-readiness is also called a *sign-gestalt-readiness.* A cluster of beliefs about something is called a *belief-value matrix.*

Sign-gestalt-expectation. Faced by a specific, concrete situation and with a readiness to react to the situation, the individual believes that if he does so act he will achieve a desired end. This is a sign-gestalt-expectation. It is also called a *means-end-expectation,* a *hypothesis,* or simply an *expectancy.*

BEHAVIOR-SUPPORTS

The environment must possess certain characteristics if a person's efforts to reach or avoid a goal are to be successful. These characteristics are called behavior-supports. There are three main classes of behavior-supports: **discriminanda, manipulanda,** and **means-end-relations.**

Discriminanda consist of the qualities or attributes of objects that enable the individual to make sensory discriminations. They are such qualities as colors, tones, odors, and tastes.

Manipulanda comprise those attributes of objects that enable a person to carry out various motor activities. These attributes are such things as length, width, weight, fluidity, and solidity.

Means-end-relations. In order for an individual to achieve a purpose, he must have some knowledge of the means for making such an achievement. Specifically, he must have some idea of the direction to take and the distance to be covered. Direction and distance are the two fundamental means-end-relations. In his later writings, Tolman referred to means-end-relations as *cognitive maps.*

LATENT LEARNING

Tolman and his students discovered that learning can take place in the absence of a motive or demand, although the learning does not manifest itself until a demand or purpose has been introduced. This learning which lies concealed until there is a reason to express it is called latent learning.

REFERENCES

Tolman, E. C. *Purposive Behavior in Rats and Men.* New York: Century, 1932.

Tolman, E. C. *Drives Toward War.* New York: Appleton-Century, 1942.

Tolman, E. C. *Collected Papers in Psychology.* Berkeley: University of California Press, 1951. (Reissued under the title *Behavior and Psychological Man: Essays in Motivation and Learning,* 1961).

Tolman, E. C. "Autobiography." In *A History of Psychology in Autobiography* (Worcester, Mass.: Clark University Press, 1952), IV, 323–329.

John B. Watson

1878–1958

Watson was the founder of behaviorism, a movement which has played a very prominent role in American psychology since its inception in 1913. Behaviorism will be defined after we have given a biographical sketch of Watson.

John Broadus Watson was born on a farm in Greenville, South Carolina, on June 9, 1878. Watson says he was an insubordinate and inferior student throughout his primary schooling. Despite his deficiencies as a pupil, he enrolled at Furman University at the age of sixteen and graduated with a master's degree five years later. He went to the University of Chicago in 1900 to study psychology and philosophy, working his way through graduate school doing whatever odd jobs he could find. Because he had trouble with the philosophy courses, he decided to major in psychology. He was awarded the Ph.D. in 1903.

He remained at Chicago for the next five years, and at the age of thirty he was invited to become professor of psychology and director of the psychological laboratory at Johns Hopkins University in Baltimore. By this time he had pretty well formulated his ideas about behaviorism, and in 1915 he presented his viewpoint in a presidential address before the American Psychological Association. It was very well received, and had an immediate impact on psychologists. His research, most of which was performed on animals and children, was interrupted by the First World War, in which he served in various capacities as a psychologist. He was not impressed by the military establishment. Of it, he wrote that he had never seen "such incompetence, such extravagance, such a group of overbearing, inferior men."

Watson's brilliant academic career ended abruptly in 1920, when he was asked to resign because he had become divorced from his wife. He moved to New York and entered the field of advertising. Within four years he had become vice president of J. Walter Thompson, one of the largest advertising agencies in the country. Watson continued to give public lectures and write popular articles and books on behaviorism. Behaviorism became widely known to the general public. In his later years, Watson withdrew almost entirely from psychological activities, devoting his time to business, his family, and his farm. He died on September 25, 1958.

Despite the fact that Watson's involvement with psychology lasted only twenty years, from his entrance as a graduate student at Chicago in 1900 to his dismissal from Johns Hopkins in 1920, no American has had a greater or more lasting effect on American psychology. **Behaviorism** was a revolutionary movement and changed the face of psychology.

BEHAVIORISM

Behaviorism is more a conception of what psychology should be than a concept. It rejects all mentalistic concepts, including consciousness, sensation, attention, will, and image. It also rejects the method of introspection which was used to analyze the structure of consciousness. In place of mentalism, Watson proposed to substitute a stimulus-response psychology. Behaviorism is often called an "objective" psychology because it deals exclusively with observable events.

Behaviorism proceeds by analyzing complex behavior into its constituent stimulus-response units. Stimulus-response is the basic unit of psychology.

The aims of behavioristic psychology are to predict and control behavior. Knowing the **stimulus,** one should be able to predict the **response.** Controlling behavior consists of determining how to get a stimulus to produce a desired response. This often requires the establishing of new connections between stimuli and responses. Connections between stimuli and responses are brought about by **frequency** and **recency.**

STIMULUS

A stimulus is any form of energy—light waves and sound waves, for example—that can excite a sense organ—the eyes or ears, for example—and eventually by way of the nervous system produce a response. A complex of stimuli acting together is called a *situation.*

RESPONSE

A response is any reaction made by a muscle or a gland. A complex of responses is called an *act.* Responses can also act as stimuli for further responses, as in playing a piece on the piano from memory.

FREQUENCY

Watson rejected the concept of reward or reinforcement used by Thorndike and Pavlov, and said that the connection between a stimulus and a response was strengthened by frequency and recency. The concept of frequency states that each time a particular stimulus calls forth a particular response, the connection between the stimulus and the response is strengthened.

RECENCY

When a number of responses are made in succession to a stimulus the connection between the last response made and the stimulus will be stronger than any of the preceding connections. That is, the most recent response to a stimulus will form a stronger connection than earlier responses to the stimulus.

REFERENCES

Watson, J. B. *Behavior: An Introduction to Comparative Psychology.* New York: Holt, Rinehart, and Winston, 1914.

Watson, J. B. *Psychology from the Standpoint of a Behaviorist.* Philadelphia: Lippincott, 1919.

Watson, J. B. *Behaviorism.* New York: People's Institute Publishing Co., 1924–1925.

Watson, J. B. "Autobiography." In *A History of Psychology in Autobiography* (Worcester, Mass.: Clark University Press, 1936), III, 271–281.

Name Index

Subject Index